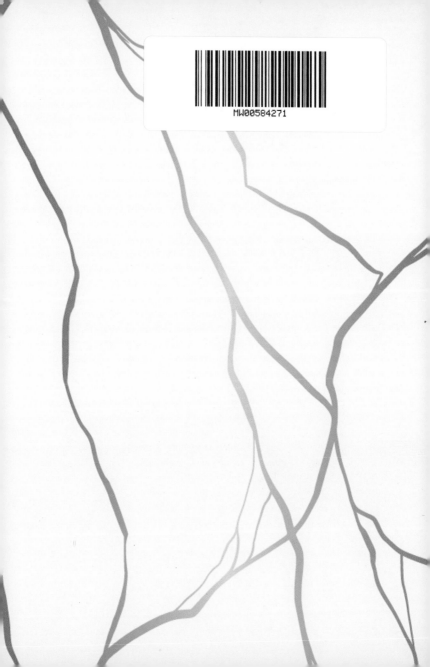

Jessica Ronne advocates for every bone-weary caregiver who feels like they have no more gas in the tank. She offers encouragement, hope, and grace to keep going.

**Lisa Whittle,** bestselling author and host of podcast *Jesus Over Everything*

This devotional provides so much more than one hundred days of hope and encouragement! It's the caregiver-focused guidebook that I've desperately needed all these years while struggling with worry and exhaustion, uncertain how to trust in God's love and purpose. I'm confident I will revisit this book again and again.

**Laurie Hellmann,** author of *Welcome to My Life: A Personal Parenting Journey Through Autism* and host of podcast *Living the Sky Life*

*Caregiving with Grit and Grace* was shared with me when I was in a desert season. God used these daily readings to breathe life and hope into my life. I was full of expectation that he would speak to me, give me what I needed, and encourage me, and he did. I have left the desert. Jessica Ronne invites us on her journey, sharing her struggles, pain, questions, and wrestling but also her unwavering faith, grace, and renewed hope. God seeks to meet each of us where we are, infusing our souls with hope and encouragement, especially on those tough days that feel like an integral part of our assignment.

**Wibke Rees,** director of Celebrate Recovery at Central Wesleyan Church

This book helps caregivers feel seen in their holy work, reminding us that blessed are the ones we care for and blessed are we who do the caring.

**Jillian Benfield,** author of *The Gift of the Unexpected: Discovering Who You Were Meant to Be When Life Goes Off Plan*

Jessica's books are honest, refreshing, faith-filled, and encouraging, and *Caregiving with Grit and Grace* is no exception. She has, once again, created a bond with her readers, as her passion for ensuring that caregivers feel seen, encouraged, and cared for shines through every page. As a caregiver herself, Jessica recognizes the unique joys and challenges of raising a child with disabilities. and caregivers will find refreshment and renewal while they learn to lean into the holy work of caring for their loved one. It is a must-read for all those who crave God's Spirit anew while serving those he entrusted to their loving care.

**Deb Stanley,** founder and CEO of Transition Bridges and author of devotional series *Taking Tea* and *The Power of Community Connectedness: Creating Lifelong Impact & Inclusion for Individuals with Disabilities*

This book is a balm to every exhausted caregiver's soul. Jessica has been a caregiver for years, and she knows how lonely and exhausting it can be. She understands the heartbreak, the disappointments, and the dark and discouraging days. In this devotional, she shares truths that point us to Jesus and help us hold on to hope while walking the often-wearying road of caregiving.

**Crystal Paine,** *New York Times* bestselling author, podcaster, and caregiver

Jessica Ronne's compassionate yet honest voice expresses truths and wisdom that caregivers need but cannot utter most days. As a therapist and professional caregiver, I value this book as a lifeline of faith, humanity, empathy, and community.

**Brenda L. Yoder,** licensed mental health counselor, therapist, school counselor, and author of *Uncomplicated: Simple Secrets for a Compelling Life*

Dear caregiver, you feel alone, exhausted, frustrated, and, at times, hopeless. As you juggle the needs of others, you're left with so little time to attend to your own. God knows that. In these pages—just one a day—you'll find small bites of nourishment, perspective, and care for your heart. Turn each page and find encouragement for your soul.

**Elisa Morgan,** president emerita of MOPS International, speaker, cohost of radio program *Discover the Word* and podcast *God Hears Her,* and author of *You Are Not Alone: 6 Affirmations from a Loving God*

Heavy, burdensome, and wearying—just a few words that describe the life of a caregiver whose heart endures the day-after-day monotony with little respite. But as you read and ponder the devotions in *Caregiving with Grit and Grace*, you will feel the heaviness lift. Jessica reminds you that Jesus sees you wrestle with life in the trenches of selflessly caring for those who cannot care for themselves and counts your work as holy. He sees each tear and hears every silent cry. Through Jessica Ronne's heartfelt, beautiful words and stories, Jesus will encourage your heart.

**Kate Battistelli,** author of *The God Dare: Will You Choose to Believe the Impossible?* and *Growing Great Kids: Partner with God to Cultivate His Purpose in Your Child's Life*

*Caregiving with Grit and Grace: 100 Days of Hope and Encouragement* by Jessica Ronne is an essential companion for anyone navigating the complex journey of caregiving. Jessica offers a wealth of wisdom, a heap of hope, and a sanctuary for the soul. Whether you're wrestling with anger, seeking peace, or yearning for a sense of community, this book guides you toward embracing your role with both the fierceness of grit and the softness of grace. A truly uplifting read for anyone caring for a loved one. It reminds us that we're not alone in our struggles and joy can be found even in the most challenging circumstances.

**Chuck Tate,** author of *41 Will Come: Holding on When Life Gets Tough— and Standing Strong until a New Day Dawns*

There is a certain fellowship of suffering that befalls those in caregiving roles. Many times, we are thrust into this role unwittingly, and sometimes we choose to step into the role. But regardless of how we got there, caring for the needs of a medically complex loved one can be a long, arduous, lonely journey. Jessica Ronne is a voice that calls us out of those dark, lonely spaces and reminds us that we aren't alone. In *Caregiving with Grit and Grace*, Jessica points us back to the Author of life, the one who sees and knows the intricacies of the hard paths we walk. She offers hope for the caregiver, the broken and overwhelmed. We are reminded of the high calling of servitude and the goodness of God. Offered in short, daily snippets for the busy caregiver, this is the book we need as we serve our loved ones.

**Kelli Stuart,** bestselling author of *Like a River from Its Course*
and *The Master Craftsman*

*Caregiving with Grit and Grace* is real, raw, and refreshing.

**Karen Vick,** content creator and caregiver

You have in your hand far more than a book—it is a sanctuary for those who do the holy work of caregiving. Not only does Jessica Ronne offer insight, wisdom, and compassion for every season of service, but her devotions also offer a safe space for both the darkest days and the moments in which hope glimmers. In these pages, there is no prescriptive language, no three-step formulas; rather, there is the voice of someone who is well-acquainted with both the fellowship of suffering and the faithfulness of God. *Caregiving with Grit and Grace* is a gift for both the caregiver and for those who walk the road with them. Thank you, Jessica. Thank you.

**Ronne Rock,** mentor, storyteller, and author of *One Woman Can
Change the World: Reclaiming Your God-Designed Influence
and Impact Right Where You Are*

This devotional sustains all those who quietly persevere in solitude and surrender. Jessica's words are a warm embrace to comfort us in the grief of our sacrifices. By her example, we, too, can receive care, knowing that we are not alone. What a glorious and desperately needed daily revelation! Because Jessica lives by the wisdom of Scripture, her words breathe life into every weary caregiver who submits to this exhausting but fulfilling calling with obedience, trust, gratitude, and hope.

**Gina Kell Spehn,** *New York Times* bestselling author of *The Color of
Rain*, writer for The Hallmark Channel's *The Color of Rain* adaptation, and
cofounder and president of New Day Foundation for Families Fighting Cancer

# CAREGIVING WITH GRIT AND GRACE

100 Days of Hope and Encouragement

## JESSICA RONNE

**BroadStreet**
PUBLISHING

BroadStreet Publishing® Group, LLC
Savage, Minnesota, USA
BroadStreetPublishing.com

Caregiving with Grit and Grace: 100 Days of Hope and Encouragement
Copyright © 2024 Jessica Ronne

9781424568413 (hardcover)
9781424568420 (ebook)

Cover and interior by Garborg Design Works | garborgdesign.com

Printed in China

24 25 26 27 28 5 4 3 2 1

To my Lucas, thank you for teaching me what it truly looks like to lay down your life for another.

To my other children, thank you for loving your brother so well and for giving me grace through my exhaustion.

To my husband, Ryan, thank you for loving Lucas as your own and for your constant encouragement to "write a devotional book."

To the families who believed in HOPE, Ryan and I are grateful for your faith in God's plan.

To those who care for a loved one, you are now a part of the fellowship of suffering. May this book encourage you to seek the one who will provide the strength to face each day and a peace that surpasses understanding.

To my Shepherd who has never left my side despite my shortcomings and failures and rotten attitude at times. Thank you for being my strength, thank you for your faithful presence, and thank you for never forsaking me as I walked through the valley of the shadow of death. To him be all glory and honor forever and ever. Amen.

# CONTENTS

# Spring

## Summer

# Fall

# FOREWORD

Of all the harsh realities of caregiving, it is the daily drag that often feels the most daunting. When another human relies on you for sustenance, health, and wholeness, there are no "skip days" or productivity hacks to let you off the hook. No. The needs of our loved ones, like the mercies of God, are new every morning. We have no choice but to pull ourselves out of bed and begin the routine anew: the meals, the appointments, the medications, and all the apprehensions that accompany them. We are the caregivers. Every day, we do what must be done.

In the midst of our marathons, we fool ourselves into thinking we have no needs of our own—that we are endlessly strong and ever-sufficient for every task on our to-do list. Then, in the dark and quiet hours, we stare at the ceiling as the reality settles into our hearts: we, too, are frail. We, too, are utterly dependent on the care and compassion of the one in whom we live and move and have our being.

Jessica Ronne has not written a meaty manifesto on the grave art of caregiving, though she probably could have. Rather, she has served up small, nourishing truths for us caregivers—each meant to be savored in the presence of God and before the rising of the sun. The entries Jessica has penned are rich and diverse. Some are challenging, some are inspiring, and some are fodder for contemplation.

All the entries, however, have one thing in common: they point upward, reminding us of our all-sufficient caregiver. That's why I'm thankful for the book you are holding. Yes, we may be weaker than we pretend to be, but our Creator never lets us down. He gave us strength yesterday, he will provide for us tomorrow, and he will certainly give us this day our daily bread.

We need not view our dependence as a shameful secret anymore, for it is that very dependence that beckons us to return to God and lift our gaze, letting him fill our cups. And out of that filling, we find the overflow to take up our service afresh with joy and purpose—with grit and grace.

**Jason Hague,** author of *Aching Joy: Following God through the Land of Unanswered Prayer*

# INTRODUCTION

*Dear Caregiver,*

Never before have I felt such conviction about the words I've written as I do about the words in this devotional. The Lord impressed upon me a high and holy calling as I spoke encouragement into spaces for weary caregivers and into my own weariness as well.

I've had quite the journey. Growing up, I was the oldest of eleven siblings and cared for them throughout childhood. Then I became a mother myself, and when doctors discovered that my second child, Lucas, experienced a stroke in utero, I learned that the long-term effects would require full-time care for the rest of his life.

Three short years later, my thirty-year-old husband, Jason, was diagnosed with a terminal brain tumor that would eventually eradicate his ability to care for himself and end in his death on August 24, 2010. I became a widow with four young children that day. Then, one year later, the Lord blessed me with a widower named Ryan who had lost his wife to cancer. We married, and I became a mother to his three grieving children too. Today, I continue to care for other caregivers through my advocacy work.

With each of these trying experiences, I felt a seasonal rhythm. The winter season represented the death of a dream or the hard truth of a diagnosis. Once I accepted my new reality, winter ushered in spring, bringing with it a lightness as I learned to find joy once again. Summer would follow, often hot and heavy, reflecting the growing intensity of treatments no longer working or caregiving demands becoming more time-consuming and exhausting. Fall represented finality, be it through death, remission, or resolution.

As I maneuvered through these seasons, I embarked on daily walks as a form of self-care. Many days, the sun shone brightly upon my face, and other days, the cold winter wind slapped itself against my exhausted body. But my prayer remained the same: *Lord, use me. Convict me of anything I need to surrender so that your message flows through me without pride or interruption.* And he did. He faithfully stripped me of anything and everything that could have possibly hindered these words. Moment by moment and step by step, I've obeyed the Lord's will, sometimes immediately and sometimes not so much.

Oswald Chambers wrote, "Why shouldn't we go through heartbreaks? Through these doorways God is opening up ways of fellowship with His Son. Most of us fall and collapse at the first grip of pain; we sit down on the threshold of God's purpose and die away of self-pity, and all so-called Christian sympathy will aid us to our death bed. But God will not. He comes with the grip of the pierced hand of His Son and says—'Enter into fellowship with Me; arise and shine.' If through a broken heart God can bring His purposes to pass in the world, then thank Him for breaking your heart."[1]

I pray that these devotions bless you as you enter the fellowship of suffering in sacred spaces of servitude. Let us not grow weary in running our races or die away of self-pity, but instead let us rise and shine! We are his hands and feet as we usher in his eternal kingdom, and his will shall be brought to fruition here as it is in heaven.

---

1   Oswald Chambers, "Ye Are Not Your Own," *My Utmost for His Highest* (Grand Rapids, MI: Discovery House, 1963), November 1, https://utmost.org/.

# WINTER

*The rain and the snow come down from heaven, and do not return
to it without watering the earth and making it bud and flourish, so
that it yields seed for the sower and bread for the eater.*

Isaiah 55:10 NIV

The winter wind whips through our life as we confront the
diagnosis of our loved one. We contemplate complex medical
language and struggle to pronounce prescriptions for medications
that held no significance to us before this season. Now, cold, hard
truths slap us in the face while medical professionals tell us our
loved one requires care.

We wrestle with feelings of denial and even depression. We
bargain with the Lord and beg him for answers, and yet we're
often met with silence. We grapple with the death of our dreams
as we realize our time now revolves around caregiving duties.
Perhaps it's the dream of raising a healthy child or growing old
with a beloved spouse or having more time with a parent than the
medical brochure implied we would. Suddenly having to navigate
a new season of uncertainty, we mourn the life we feel we should
have had as we enter a fellowship of suffering with our loved one.

During the winter months, we recall that the snow provides
moisture, and moisture produces growth, and growth will
eventually provide nourishment to those who desperately yearn
for hope. Stay faithful. Winter doesn't last forever.

# OUR LORD'S PRESENCE

*"My soul is overwhelmed with sorrow to the point of death.*
*Stay here and keep watch with me."*
MATTHEW 26:38 NIV

The doctor stretched out her arm and drew circles on top of circles on the whiteboard, an illustration of how she viewed my unborn baby's predicament: a presumed diagnosis of a stroke in utero. I sat there feeling like a child failing miserably at a particular subject in school, but the subject I was failing in was pregnancy.

My figurative teacher drew a large head to represent the accumulated fluid and then continued to draw more circles around that head, signifying swelling as the amount of fluid increased. I half expected her to write the word *BOOM* and draw scribbles depicting chaos after the head would ultimately explode. She didn't. She simply said, "If I were you, I would take care of it and try again."

That was the day I unknowingly became a forever caregiver. Throughout the remainder of my pregnancy with Lucas, my soul was overwhelmed with sorrow. I cried out, *Lord! Please take this cup from me!* But all I heard was silence.

Jesus knew my pain, and he knows yours too. He's with us during the unexpected diagnoses, the treatments, the doctors' appointments, and the agonizing decisions. He's present in the sleepless nights. He enters our fellowship of suffering and keeps vigil beside us. He does for us what he asked his disciples to do for him. He stays with us, keeps watch over us, and comforts us. In their human frailty, the disciples failed him. But Jesus will never fail us. He will stay and keep watch beside us—always.

*Jesus, in this new caregiving journey, I thank you for your continuous presence.*

# SUFFICIENT GRACE

*"My grace is sufficient for you,*
*for my power is made perfect in weakness."*
2 CORINTHIANS 12:9 NIV

I hesitantly walked into a healing class and took my seat. A few weeks prior, I learned about the class from a church bulletin. It was led by a Spirit-filled doctor who'd been saved in his youth from a life of sex, drugs, and rock 'n' roll and converted into a larger-than-life, "Hallelujah, praise the Lord" type of personality. His energy was exactly what I needed at that time in my life. I was desperate for a miracle for my unborn baby and willing to set aside everything to pursue it.

An older, heavyset man named Walter sat beside me. He was a gentle, old soul and provided a sense of calm and belonging. Yet for all his kindness, Walter's presence in this class posed a personal conflict in me. He needed healing for type 2 diabetes, most likely brought on by his obesity.

As we prayed for his healing, I felt sad and awkward for him. In my prideful arrogance I thought, *Walter should pray to overcome the sin of gluttony.* I was almost jealous of him and thought, *If I could fix my problem, I wouldn't be here. Life would be easier if I could simply take matters into my own hands and heal this baby instead of relying on God for miraculous healing.*

A few months after the class, I read that Walter had passed away from diabetic complications. His death sobered me and made me realize how much Walter relied on God in his weakness. He loved the Lord, and he was right to rely on him. I wondered if I did too.

Do you rely on the Lord for your strength, or do you struggle with urges to control things, like I do? Release any perceived notions that you have control, for his power is made perfect in our weakness.

> *Lord, may I rely on your love and provision and not lean on my own understanding and strength.*

## 3

# ANGER LEADS TO HARM

*Stop being angry! Turn from your rage!*
*Do not lose your temper—it only leads to harm.*
PSALM 37:8 NLT

When I was weeks away from giving birth to Lucas, my family threw a joint baby shower for my aunt and me. My aunt had recently married, and she was quick to get pregnant since her childbearing window was narrowing. She was forty-one and had a perfectly healthy baby inside her womb; I was twenty-seven and had a baby declared terminal inside mine. It felt like a cruel joke.

No one knew if they should congratulate me or grieve with me at this awkward event, and I had to tiptoe around everyone else's discomfort. I eventually ran to the bathroom to slow my quickening breath and to stop the shaking that had overcome my body. I silently screamed into the mirror, *It's not fair, Lord! I hate this!*

It's natural to get angry when life doesn't feel fair, which can be a daily occurrence as a caregiver. But according to the Lord, holding anger in your heart only leads to harm. It didn't solve or change anything when I gave in to my intense anger that day; I only missed out on the blessing of a baby shower. Nineteen years later, I can see the Lord's hand over my life, but in my anger, I could only see unfairness. Release your anger to the Lord.

*Lord, take my anger and replace it with your peace.*

# 4

# WORK AS WORSHIP

.

*The L*ORD *God took the man*
*and put him in the Garden of Eden*
*to work it and take care of it.*

GENESIS 2:15 NIV

$A$ s the date of my C-section approached, I began to fret about the lack of time I would have available for the Lord after the baby was born. I spent most of my time during pregnancy reading Scripture, listening to worship music, and pressing into the Lord's provision through prayer. My soul yearned for this constant renewal through these disciplines, and when I realized that my baby's birth was going to hinder this sweet time of communion, I became a bit panicky.

*Lord*, I whispered, *I need this with you. I need to have my soul drenched with your presence. I need to continuously be enshrined in your love.*

*Yes,* he whispered back. *The drenching of your spirit was necessary for a time, but when your baby arrives, you will worship through the care of this child whom I have called you to raise.*

We often think of worship as singing, dancing, praying, lifting holy hands, and reading our Bibles, and yes, those are beautiful and necessary forms of worship. There is a time to be saturated in this way, and then there is the act of worship through our work in the same way that Adam and Eve were called to work in the garden.

I had to shift my priorities after Lucas was born because he required never-ending care, but because I had poured my soul into praise and prayer in the months prior, the Lord equipped me to accomplish the task of raising my special boy.

*Lord, help me to see my work as worship.*

## 5

# FIND FREEDOM

*About midnight Paul and Silas were praying and singing hymns
to God, and the other prisoners were listening to them. Suddenly
there was such a violent earthquake that the foundations of the
prison were shaken. At once all the prison doors flew open, and
everyone's chains came loose.*

ACTS 16:25–26 NIV

W hen I was seven months pregnant and had already received
the hopeless diagnosis for my unborn child, I attended a healing
service at church. When the pastor called forward those who
needed healing, I waddled down, tears streaming and mascara
smearing, and knelt at the altar. With my hands raised in praise, I
begged Jesus to heal my baby. My desperation allowed me to set
aside my ego, which was ultimately an act of surrender.

Perhaps Paul and Silas felt desperate when they were
imprisoned. They probably wondered if they were going to die,

and their desperation allowed them to set aside their egos. Their surrender to God led to a release of control, and they sang and prayed at the top of their lungs. Their surrender released action in the eternal realm and brought freedom!

My praise didn't bring the exact healing that I desired for my unborn baby, but it did provide a peace that surpassed understanding. In that peace, I found freedom; the garment of praise replaced my spirit of heaviness (Isaiah 61:3). Our praise frees us from our inclinations to attempt to control a situation, and we can find that freedom only by placing our trust in the Lord.

*Father, grant me your peace through my*
*act of worship.*

# 6

# DON'T COMPLAIN

*The children of Israel said unto them, Would to God we had died by*
*the hand of the LORD in the land of Egypt, when we sat by the flesh*
*pots, and when we did eat bread to the full; for ye have brought us*
*forth into this wilderness, to kill this whole assembly with hunger.*

EXODUS 16:3 KJV

I was home with Lucas, my beautiful miracle baby, for a few weeks
when the exhaustion, frustration, and anxiety kicked in. Lucas did
not sleep. My husband, Jason, and I tried everything we could think
of, but this child woke up every twenty minutes or so. I was so tired
I couldn't see straight.

Sleep deprivation quickly leads a person to irrational thoughts,
and I started to resent that I had been chosen to be Lucas's mom.
In my quietest hours of exhaustion, I wondered, *Why did I pray so*
*hard for this child's life when it's so difficult to be his mother?*

My despair led me to my Bible one weary morning, and I landed on Exodus 16. The Israelites had been rescued from their bondage in Egypt, and as I hazily reread the familiar story, the Lord had words to say to me: *I delivered the Israelites from Pharaoh, and all they did was complain in the desert. I delivered your baby, and all you do is complain about him.*

*I'm sorry,* I whispered. *Lord, help me to rely on you for my strength. Help me to joyfully obey, and please grant me the rest I need. I repent of my attitude and resolve to trust in your plan for my life.*

*Lord, may I restrain myself from complaining and instead trust in you.*

# 7

# CHOOSE YES

*They compelled a passerby, Simon of Cyrene, who was coming in*
*from the country, the father of Alexander and Rufus, to carry his cross.*

MARK 15:21 ESV

Do you realize that Simon became a caregiver to Jesus? He was simply going about his day when the soldiers abruptly picked him out of a crowd to carry the Lord's cross. What an honor! But did Simon see it that way? What if he had argued or come up with an excuse? What if he had run away?

Simon probably didn't have much of a say in the matter, much like we often don't have a say in our caregiving duties. Of course, someone else could have been chosen, but then Simon would have missed out on the blessing of caring for Jesus only hours before the Savior's sacrifice for humanity. The weight of humanity potentially hinged on Simon's *yes* in that sacred moment.

Simon's *yes* became a public caregiving moment, not unlike many of our moments with our loved ones. My son Lucas can be messy, loud, and aggressive. He drools sometimes, drinks from a sippy cup, and the whole diaper issue can make outings stressful and uncomfortable. I'll bet Simon felt similar as he carried a 110-pound cross on his back. Sweat dripping down his brow, stumbling, fumbling, maybe murmuring a curse or two under his breath, Simon cared for the Messiah during Jesus' final hours on earth.

God could have chosen anyone to care for your loved one, but God chose you. He anointed you for the task. Simon said *yes*, and in doing so, he became our Lord's caregiver. This alone should inspire us to say *yes* when God calls us to care for others.

*Lord, may I always choose yes.*

# 8

# LIE DOWN IN PEACE

*In peace I will lie down and sleep,*
*for you alone, LORD, make me dwell in safety.*
PSALM 4:8 NIV

When Lucas was a young child, I often bristled whenever someone brought up the topic of sleep. It wasn't that I didn't want to sleep; it was Lucas who didn't want to sleep! Many caregivers are familiar with the sleep deprivation that comes with never-ending tasks.

Sleep deprivation is a type of difficult you don't even want to talk about because by acknowledging your exhaustion, you feel helpless, and then the tears begin to flow because you're just so dang tired. As caregivers, we don't even have time for our own tears, do we? We don't have time to grieve. We simply keep moving to the detriment of our health.

The Bible has a lot to say about the precious commodity of sleep and encourages us to pursue the rest we need. During those early years with Lucas, I had to first be honest about my exhaustion, and this honest admission led me to ask a trusted couple if they would watch our kids so that Jason and I could get away for a weekend of respite.

There is simply no way we can be the best version of ourselves when we are continuously deprived of rest. And we aren't doing our loved ones any favors by jeopardizing our health, as if our sleep deprivation is some kind of badge of honor. We cannot walk confidently into our holy calling of caregiving without the rest we need.

*Father, send people into my life who can offer me a reprieve from my caregiving duties.*

# 9

# RELEASE ANXIETY

*Do not be anxious about anything, but in every situation, by prayer and petition, with thanksgiving, present your requests to God.*

PHILIPPIANS 4:6 NIV

I'm really good at revving up my anxiety by anticipating and solving imaginary problems. After Lucas was diagnosed in utero, I got to work. I researched potential issues, worst-case scenarios, and then therapies, treatments, and options to mitigate worst-case scenarios. The purpose behind all my research was to ensure my one and only plan for Lucas (and me): to lead healthy, normal lives. But the Lord said, *Nope. That's not my plan.*

None of my exhaustive research or careful planning helped us avoid even a single issue. Instead, I received the equivalent of the worst-case scenario, which was the best-case scenario in the eyes of my Savior, who wanted to use the experience of being Lucas's mom to make me more Christlike and to bring glory to his name.

The Lord continues to convict me that my habit of dwelling on imaginary problems can quickly develop into a habit of idolatry. When I worship at the altar of "Jessica grasping for control" rather than thankfully submitting and presenting my requests to God, my anticipating and planning are exactly that—idols. When my faith in Google, humans, or myself replaces my faith in the Lord, that's a problem.

We long for others to see our Savior's love through us, and this natural manifestation occurs only when we release our problems to the one who is truly in control.

*Lord, I release my anxiety as I present my problems*
*to you.*

# HOPE IN JESUS

*"His name will be the hope of all the world."*
MATTHEW 12:21 NLT

After Jason was diagnosed with brain cancer, I felt as if I had a target on my back that read, "Here's Jess Ronne. Give her loved ones all the brain issues in the world." I didn't even have enough fight in me to be angry those first few days. I was simply hopeless and sad. I had three children under the age of five and a husband with a brain tumor.

Jason saw how dejected I was and invited my friend over. We talked and sipped our tea, and she asked if she could pray for me. When she prayed, she whispered, "Jesus, Jesus, Jesus," and as she said his name, I found myself agreeing and echoing her sentiment. As we declared the name of Jesus, my heart felt lighter, and my hope began to return.

Caregivers, we need hope more than anything. Hope is what gets us out of bed every day to accomplish the monotonous and mundane. Hope is what prevents us from running away or throwing our hands up in despair. Hope is what makes everything we do worthwhile—hope in eternity, hope for ourselves, and hope for our loved one.

Matthew 12:21 states, "His name will be the hope of all the world" (NLT). Whisper the name of Jesus in your quiet moments of despair or declare his name aloud as you wrestle with feelings of doubt and anger. His name is the key to our hope.

*Jesus, I speak your name over my situation.*
*In you alone I find my hope.*

# 11

# TRADE WORRIES FOR JOY

*"I tell you, do not worry about your life."*
MATTHEW 6:25 NIV

Worry is a veiled attempt at control. Does that statement register with you? I know it does for me. I worried about Lucas's health, especially when I was pregnant with him. I worried about him reaching milestones, about my husband's cancer treatments, about my life as a widow, and about the future—that's been a big worry.

My worry brought forth a "speak it and believe it" mentality. I made fervent attempts to win the Almighty's approval so that he would grant me a miracle, as if I could somehow manipulate the God of the universe. What a ridiculous thought!

It's been a long road for me to reach the point of understanding that worry is a manipulation tactic and a desperate attempt to determine the outcome, the outcome that we want. And it never works. This truth has been a hard and holy lesson for me throughout the years.

When our worry is at its peak in that frantic, peaceless state—buying all the supplements, joining all the support groups, and living in fight-or-flight mode—that's exactly when we need to lean into the Lord and his comfort. He promises to bring us joy despite whatever it is we're going through.

> *Lord, I release my desire to worry my way to a favorable outcome, and instead I allow you to console me.*

# 12

# IT IS FINISHED

*When Jesus had received the sour wine, He said, "It is finished!"*
*And bowing His head, He yielded up His spirit.*

JOHN 19:30 BSB

Do you sometimes feel like God ignores your cries for help? I know I do. I remember writhing in agony, barely able to catch my breath, as I begged the Lord to heal Jason after his cancer diagnosis. All I heard was silence.

I interpreted the silence to mean that God didn't care or had forgotten about me. Or perhaps the problems of the world had become too heavy for his sovereign shoulders to carry, so he stopped worrying about how I was doing.

I would have gladly accepted any kind of response, even a *no*, over the deafening silence that I received. I couldn't take control. I couldn't fix anything, and I couldn't get a head start on grief. I simply had to be still and trust, and I hated it, if I'm being honest.

Do you ever feel the same? You beg for a response, but all you hear is silence? No answers, no still, small voice, no signs, nothing, and you wonder if God even remembers that you exist. Take heart! God was also silent when his Son begged him to intervene: "Father...Take this cup from me" (Mark 14:36 NIV). Help only arrived when Jesus declared, "It is finished!" and entered eternity.

We may not see our reward on this side of eternity, but we will someday.

*Father, thank you for the gift of our eternal reward.*

# 13

# MULTIPLY MY NEEDS

*Jesus then took the loaves, gave thanks,
and distributed to those who were seated
as much as they wanted.
He did the same with the fish.*
JOHN 6:11 NIV

The biggest commodities I lack as a caregiver are time and sleep, and I bet you can relate. Caregiving duties require a lot of energy, and, for my situation anyway, "a lot" translates to 24/7 care: early mornings, night-time wakings, and evenings when Lucas doesn't want to go to sleep on my timetable. I've lived in a state of exhaustion for over nineteen years. It's difficult to be productive when you're just...so...tired.

As I read today's verse one morning, I realized I had the authority to ask the Lord to multiply these precious commodities—to multiply my time and sleep just like he multiplied the fish and the loaves. I set aside my Bible and prayed, *Lord, please multiply my time today. Give me supernatural strength to accomplish the hard and holy tasks that lie before me. And Lord, please multiply my sleep tonight and in your great mercy, my son's sleep as well.* That night, Lucas slept straight through without waking a single time. All it took was my humble ask.

As Jesus told us, "Ask, and you will receive" (John 16:24 ESV). The Lord is faithful to provide. What do you need multiplied in your life? Ask with expectancy and faith and then watch the Lord move.

*Thank you, Lord, for providing everything I need.*

# 14

# HOLY WORK

*"Now that I, your Lord and Teacher, have washed your feet, you
also should wash one another's feet. I have set you an example that
you should do as I have done for you."*

JOHN 13:14–15 NIV

A few years ago, I hung a wooden sign above Lucas's bed that
simply states, "This is holy work." It serves as my daily reminder
that caring for him is holy.

Jesus would have joyfully cared for my son. Jesus would have
bathed him, dressed him, and changed him. Jesus would have fed
him, wiped the crumbs from his face, and crouched down to lace
his shoes. Jesus would have sat beside him and patiently explained
(again and again) how to navigate his iPad. And Jesus would have
deemed each of these caring actions as holy work.

Jesus sought out the company of the marginalized: the tax
collector, the beggar, and the leper, and not only did he seek out

their presence, but he also sought to touch them spiritually and physically. He washed their feet and told us to do the same—to do as he has done for us. My goodness, that's a heavy calling!

What an honor it is that we, too, as caregivers, accomplish holy work when we lay down our agendas to serve our loved ones. Some might even say that caring for an individual who could not exist or survive without loving intervention from others is the holiest work that we can accomplish on this side of eternity.

*Lord, it is an honor to become more Christlike by caring for those who are most vulnerable in my life.*

# 15

# A SERVANT FOR CHRIST

*"Whoever wants to be first must be your slave—*
*just as the Son of Man did not come to be served, but to serve,*
*and to give his life as a ransom for many."*

MATTHEW 20:27–28 NIV

The words in today's verses are so contrary to what we want
to experience in life. We strive to get ahead, to serve ourselves,
to serve our families, to make more money, to make a name for
ourselves, and to be recognized and admired. Sure, some of
those aspirations are worthy, but they aren't nearly as worthy as
what Jesus calls us to strive for. Jesus states that greatness in the
kingdom of God comes from laying down our desire for self, laying
down our ego, and becoming a slave to others.

The word *slave* kind of throws me because of the atrocities
of slavery. It's a word embedded with so much pain. Still, when I
dwell on the reality of our circumstances, I remember that our lives

as caregivers are not our own. We *are* bound to our loved one's schedules and appointments and sleep habits and medications and food preferences and dietary limitations.

My life is not my own when it comes to caring for Lucas. He often can't be reasoned with, and whatever he wants, he wants immediately. So yes, I suppose that makes me Lucas's slave in the same way it's used in Matthew 20:27–28, but if that helps me become more like Jesus, then so be it. I will give my life as a ransom to serve my son and, in turn, to serve my Savior.

*Lord, I set aside my ego and become a slave for others so that I may serve you.*

# 16

# MORE VALUABLE THAN A SPARROW

*"Look at the birds of the air: they neither sow nor reap nor gather into barns, and yet your heavenly Father feeds them. Are you not of more value than they?"*

MATTHEW 6:26 ESV

Jason and I were watching our favorite television show when we heard a loud chirping coming from the deck. After a bit of investigative work, we discovered that our cat had found a sparrow, and the poor bird was nearly dead. Caleb, our six-year-old son, entered the room, and after some deliberation, he wrapped the bird in a bath towel and carried it to the top of his swing set to keep it safe for the night.

Jason and I went to bed, and I prayed for that dumb bird all night. Honestly, it was a relief to beg God to heal something besides Jason, who was deteriorating quickly because of the cancer treatments. The next morning, we discovered the sparrow had died during the night.

I was so irritated. *God, why couldn't you have just healed the dumb bird?* I questioned. Later that day, we also learned that Jason's cancer was no longer responding to treatments. I sighed and remembered the sparrow and God's promise that we are more valuable than the birds.

It's difficult to trust God's plan at times, especially when it seems contrary to what the plan should be. However, when we recall his deep abiding love for us and that "all things work together for the good of those who love God" (Romans 8:28 CSB), we remember that we carry far more value than the sparrows, and he will faithfully provide.

*Lord, I trust your provision.*

# 17

# ALL MY HEART

*Trust in the LORD with all your heart and lean not on your own understanding; in all your ways submit to him, and he will make your paths straight.*

PROVERBS 3:5–6 NIV

W hen my daughter Annabelle was seven years old, I explained to her that instead of questioning every single request I make of her, she should instead trust my love for her. Rather than giving me a million excuses, she should simply obey.

As I explained all this to her, a still, small voice whispered Proverbs 3:5 to me: *Trust in the LORD with all your heart and lean not on your own understanding.* It's funny how the Lord often convicts me with my little speeches.

I sometimes struggle to trust the Lord's heart for my life. I have felt overwhelmed with duties and the fear that my entire life will center around caregiving. I cared for my eleven siblings while growing up; I care for Lucas and my seven other children, and I care for other caregiving parents through my advocacy work. It feels like a lot of caregiving for one person to handle, like I was called to a great deal of obedience that most other people don't have piled on their plates.

*Trust me, with all your heart,* the voice continued to whisper. *Trust me like you want your daughter to trust you. Trust my heart for you, and instead of questioning or giving me a million excuses, I want you to simply obey.* I sighed in surrender and whispered, *Yes, Lord, I will trust you.*

*Lord, help me to trust in you with all my heart.*

# 18

# MOUNTAINTOP MOMENTS

*After six days Jesus took Peter, James, and John his brother,*
*led them up on a high mountain by themselves; and He was*
*transfigured before them. His face shone like the sun, and His*
*clothes became as white as the light.*

MATTHEW 17:1–2 NKJV

Jesus experienced one mountaintop moment in his lifetime when he was transfigured before a small group of people. Just one. He spent the rest of his ministry in the valley of service to others. He served tax collectors, prostitutes, and sinners; he fed people and healed the lepers and the blind.

We live for the mountaintop moments: the promotion, the viral post, and hearing the words, "Your baby is alive!" or "We resected all of the tumor!" These moments keep us going, propel us forward, and provide hope. We yearn for more of these highlight reels in our life, but we must also remember that the God of the universe, who lived among us for thirty-three years, had only *one* mountaintop moment.

Sure, the occasional mountaintop moment strengthens our faith as we rise to meet our Maker, but the valley is where we humbly become more like him. Oswald Chambers wrote, "We see his glory on the mount, but we never live for his glory there."[2] Our singular pursuit should be to serve others in both the mountaintop moments and the hidden valleys. Jesus lived a life of servitude, and as his followers, we should do the same.

*Lord, may I humbly serve in quiet and unseen spaces*
*and not seek out mountaintop moments for myself.*

---

2  Chambers, "Sphere of Humiliation," *My Utmost for His Highest*, October 2.

# 19

# DESIRE VERSUS DUTY

*"Father, if you are willing, take this cup from me;*
*yet not my will, but yours be done."*

LUKE 22:42 NIV

After doctors told me that my unborn baby would most likely die, I entered an intense period of prayer. I prayed fervently that the Lord would not only spare my baby but that he would also grant complete and total healing. After giving birth to Lucas, I realized that God had not met my desire for complete healing; my duty was to raise a fragile child who would require extensive care for the rest of his life.

Desire versus duty. Each one of us will face these decisions throughout our lives: choosing between that which we desire to do and that which God calls us to do. I desired to raise a typical, healthy child, but God called me to raise a profoundly disabled child who required lifelong care. I had two choices. I could have abdicated my duty and run away, given Lucas up for adoption, or terminated the pregnancy, or I could have chosen to obey and accept my duty.

After praying three times and desiring a different way—an alternate plan to save humanity—Jesus surrendered to his Father's will and accepted his duty to die on the cross. Jesus could have run away and said, *Nope, I'm not doing that. Dying on a cross is too much to bear*, but his desire and love for humanity allowed him to follow through on his duty—just like our love and desire for our loved ones allow us to say yes to our marching orders.

*Lord, I surrender my desires and will obey the duty*
*you have called me to.*

# 20

# SIMPLE SELF-CARE

*He came to a broom bush, sat down under it and prayed that he might die. "I have had enough, LORD," he said. "Take my life; I am no better than my ancestors."*

1 KINGS 19:4 NIV

Elijah experienced a hallelujah victory moment when he reigned down fire from heaven and blasted the prophets of Baal out of this world. Instead of riding high on the momentum of this miraculous event and spiritually hot doggin' with the Lord, he sat down under a bush and asked to die. And how embarrassing it is that I have often acted in a similar manner.

We have our hallelujah moments as caregivers when we receive a breakthrough or an answer to prayer or when we move off a waitlist and into an opportunity or when doctors declare our loved one is cancer free. We're high-fiving and dancing with glee, and then the next moment or day or week, we're right back down in the dumps again, complaining about our life. We might not literally ask to die like Elijah did, but our poor attitudes lead us to act half dead.

Elijah's story continues, *He slept and ate* (a major simplification of the text), *and he felt better.* So often we, too, will feel better if we simply take a nap or eat some food. If you're feeling worn out and half dead, take stock of your life. Do you need a nap or a nourishing meal? Be honest and then prioritize your needs.

*Lord, help me make time to prioritize*
*my own well-being.*

# 21

# SURRENDER TO HIS WILL

*Jacob was left alone, and a man wrestled with him till daybreak…he touched the socket of Jacob's hip so that his hip was wrenched as he wrestled with the man.*

GENESIS 32:24–25 NIV

During Jason's final days, others praised me for my strength and faith, but I struggled mightily with the Lord's decisions. That struggle manifested itself through anger, clouding me from the truth that my heart was shattering into a million pieces. I raged and begged God to heal my husband.

I trusted God's sovereignty, but I wasn't convinced that he understood my situation. Perhaps I could explain it to him so that he would finally see that I needed him to completely heal my husband. Maybe I could somehow twist the arm of the Almighty, wrestle with him, and modify his will. Maybe, just maybe, I could get my way. I wrestled for three years until the final weeks of Jason's life, when I finally surrendered and declared, *You are God, and I am not. Blessed be your name.*

I don't believe the Lord faulted me one single bit for questioning and wrestling with him. I don't believe periods of wrestling diminish our faith either. In fact, I think wrestling is sometimes necessary.

However, when we wrestle with God, we must also accept the consequences that often manifest themselves in some form of a limp. My limp was exhaustion. I had spent what little energy I had wrestling rather than surrendering.

Our limps may look different, but we must remember the consequences of questioning the Lord rather than obeying him.

*Lord, help me to have the courage to immediately surrender to your will.*

# 22

# THE LORD IS MY SHEPHERD

*The LORD is my shepherd; I shall not want.*
*He maketh me to lie down in green pastures:*
*he leadeth me beside the still waters.*
*He restoreth my soul.*
PSALM 23:1–3 KJV

In 2004, I was told my unborn child would die, and in 2009, I was told the same about my husband. During those difficult months in 2004, I allowed Psalm 23 to permeate my being.

I invited the Shepherd into my pain, and he guided me onto paths of righteousness. He restored my soul as we walked beside quiet waters. I cried out to him, and even though I walked through the valley of the shadow of death with my unborn child, I trusted God's lead and rested in the knowledge that goodness and mercy were not only mine but also promised to my baby.

But 2009 was different. I was exhausted from caring for a dying husband, and I used it as an excuse to not seek the Lord regularly while walking through the valley of the shadow of death—again. I ignored the Shepherd's lead and attempted to control the situation. I raged against the injustice he had allowed in my life. I resisted his lead to still waters and declined his invitation to be anointed with healing oil.

My experiences in both 2004 and 2009 were opportunities to be led and comforted by the Shepherd. One main difference between them was my choice to stay beside the Shepherd or to leave his side. When I was pregnant with Lucas, I leaned into the Lord's strength to carry me through that difficult time. With Jason, I leaned into my own strength and, out of anger, rejected the Shepherd.

Weary caregiver, stay beside the Shepherd. The peace he offers far outweighs the stress that comes from attempting to control your circumstances. Let him lead, restore, anoint, and comfort you. Let him shepherd your heart.

*Father, I accept you as my Shepherd.*
*Lead and guide me.*

# 23

# MINISTRY IN A FOREIGN LAND

*Paul went in and prayed for him, and laying his hands on him,*
*he healed him. Then all the other sick people on the island came*
*and were healed.*

ACTS 28:8–9 NLT

I'm quite certain it wasn't on Paul's agenda on this particular day
to become caught in an intense storm at sea that would eventually
capsize his boat and wash him up on the shore of an unfamiliar
island.

I read this passage and think, *Yikes, that's definitely a day*
*gone south.* However, we soon discover that Paul was healing and
praying for the islanders! These were folks he never would have met
had he not boarded that boat and survived a shipwreck. This story
hits close to home.

I have found myself in the role of advocate in service to
caregivers because I was obedient and entered a symbolic

boat when I said *yes* to being Lucas's mom. And since that yes, I've endured many storms and landed on a foreign island, a caregiving island, a sacred space of ministry and a place of beauty and transformative power manifested through the fellowship of suffering. It is because of my symbolic shipwreck that I have the honor of sharing my story and offering hope to other caregivers in seemingly hopeless circumstances.

What shipwreck landed you on an unfamiliar island? Cancer? Special needs? Death? Are you allowing God to use your shipwreck for his glory as you minister to people you would have never met had you not endured the storm?

*Thank you, Lord, for using the circumstances in my life to minister to people I never would have had the opportunity to meet had I not weathered the storm.*

24

# ACCEPT COMFORT

*They sat down with him on the ground seven days and seven nights, and no one spoke a word to him, for they saw that his grief was very great.*

JOB 2:13 NKJV

A few days after Jason's death, I was busy planning his funeral and celebration of life, securing his death certificate, and filing insurance claims. All necessary obligations. My days were filled to the brim with duties. My nights, however, were...well, different.

After the children went to bed, I was forced to confront the loneliness of my new reality. I couldn't hide behind busyness, and I came to hate the quietness, the stillness. I often scrolled on Facebook far too late into the night to avoid feeling lonely and to avoid yet another night of insomnia.

One night during this same difficult, awkward week, I heard a knock on my door around eight in the evening. I opened my door and was surprised to see one of my best friends standing there with a pint of chocolate ice cream in her hands. The tears began to flow.

"I've come to sit with you," she said. We scooped ice cream into bowls and sat together at the kitchen table. We exchanged just a few words, but she sat with me in my pain. Her presence became my comfort.

Whatever grief you're facing, allow others to comfort you.

*Father, thank you for the gift of friends who sit with me in my grief and who offer the community of care.*

# 25

# REMAIN IN ME

*"Remain in me, as I also remain in you. No branch can bear fruit by itself; it must remain in the vine. Neither can you bear fruit unless you remain in me."*

JOHN 15:4 NIV

I've shared that anger was my go-to emotion when Jason was diagnosed with cancer, but my attempts to control the situation without the Lord only led to exhaustion and stress. When Lucas ended up in the ICU for six weeks in 2019 due to a shunt malfunction, I was determined to remain in Christ and keep my peace despite the extremely challenging circumstances.

I read uplifting Scripture, prioritized sleep, and scheduled self-care through daily walks during which I would pray. I engrafted myself into the Lord's provision just as Jesus remained one with the Father in whatever circumstances he faced—even as he agonized in the garden, even as Satan tempted him in the desert, and even as the nails pierced his hands upon the cross.

It's a choice to remain grafted into our Savior's provision and love. We can choose to try to control everything in our own strength (though we will fail), or we can surrender and allow the strength of our heavenly Father to carry us. If we remain faithfully grafted into the Lord, the moisture from the winter season will bring growth as we move forward into the beauty of spring.

What choice will you make as you continue to care for your loved one?

*Father, may I remain engrafted in your provision for my strength and well-being as I care for my loved ones and move into spring.*

# SPRING

*The winter is past; the rain is over and gone. The flowers appear on the earth, the time of singing has come, and the voice of the turtledove is heard in our land. The fig tree ripens its figs, and the vines are in blossom; they give forth fragrance.*

SONG OF SOLOMON 2:11–13 ESV

Ah, it's spring. We've accepted our role as a caregiver, and we find our groove in this new season.

We instill rhythms and routines as we emerge from despair and discover joy again, recognizing that our situation is different but not less than. Life begins to bud as we celebrate growth, milestones, and the wins that we accomplished. Therapies or treatments become our normal, and we even carve out a bit of cherished time for ourselves in the middle of the chaos.

Life is more manageable. We release control and embrace hope while we watch buds turn to blossoms.

# 26

# FIX YOUR GAZE

*"Come, " [Jesus] said. Then Peter got down out of the boat, walked on the water and came toward Jesus. But when he saw the wind, he was afraid and, beginning to sink, cried out, "Lord, save me!"*
MATTHEW 14:29–30 NIV

When Jason battled cancer, I focused on the cancer and not on my Savior. I had moments when my focus turned to the Lord, but generally, I was focused on how sick my husband was, how overwhelmed I was, and how my husband might die.

I was in a metaphorical boat with my Lord. He said *Come, step out of the boat and walk a painful cancer path.* Instead of locking my eyes on Jesus, I often looked down at the raging waters and began to sink, just like Peter did when he doubted the Lord's provision.

Jesus was merciful and pulled me (and Peter) back up to safety, but oh, how much heartache and energy I could have saved myself had I continuously fixated on Jesus and not on my circumstances—if I had simply removed all doubt and moved forward in faith when the Lord said, *Come.*

It's easy to fixate on our caregiving circumstances because they are hard! It's easy to feel sorry for ourselves, but think about how much time and energy we could preserve if we simply chose to never take our eyes off our Lord. Don't stare at the storm. Fix your gaze on the Creator of the storm, and he will save you.

*Father, we fix our eyes firmly on you. Thank you for saving us when we forget and focus on our storm.*

# 27

# TAKE ROOT IN YOUR JOURNEY

*"Consider the lilies of the field, how they grow:*
*they neither toil nor spin."*

MATTHEW 6:28 NKJV

**M**y second husband, Ryan, and I managed to escape into the mountains for a couple of days just the two of us, and on a hike one morning, we found a beautiful meadow full of wildflowers. The beauty of it took my breath away, and while marveling at their splendor, I realized that wildflowers don't strive to be anything but wildflowers.

We don't see wildflowers chasing after YouTube fame or studying to become doctors. Wildflowers simply exist as they are, reflecting their Creator's will and remaining present and active in their purpose set before them. They take root wherever they are placed, and then they blossom into the fullness and splendor of all their wildflower glory.

God promises the same provision for us if we take root in our circumstances. This rootedness requires us to make a conscious choice to stop wallowing in the *what-ifs* of the past and the unfairness of the disease or diagnosis. Instead, we must embrace a spirit of gratitude and surrender to our present.

If we firmly root ourselves in the knowledge that our caregiving duties are the Lord's calling for this season and allow ourselves to go deep into the caregiving journey, this rootedness will lead to growth, blossoming, and eventual beauty—for us and for the one we serve.

*Father, I choose to take root where you have placed me.*

# 28

# CARE IS COMMUNAL

*The LORD said to Moses: "Bring me seventy of Israel's elders who are known to you as leaders and officials among the people. Have them come to the tent of meeting, that they may stand there with you. I will come down and speak with you there, and I will take some of the power of the Spirit that is on you and put it on them. They will share the burden of the people with you so that you will not have to carry it alone."*

NUMBERS 11:16–17 NIV

Are you familiar with martyr-caregiver syndrome? *No one can accomplish tasks like me!* Or, *If I allow someone to help, they'll just mess it up.* Believe me, I've been the queen bee of this club. After an intense round of chemo, Jason had to drive me to the emergency room for an uncontrollable panic attack. I couldn't catch my breath—a direct result of my martyr-caregiver syndrome.

Even Moses struggled with the martyr-caregiver syndrome. Apparently, it didn't dawn on him to ask for help. The Lord had to tell him, *Hey, Moses! Bring me seventy leaders. I'm going to anoint them to help you because you shouldn't carry this burden alone* (Numbers 11:16–17).

We are wired to share our burdens communally, but this requires us to make the decision to release control, which is difficult to do when it involves the care of a loved one. And you're right— no one will provide care or accomplish tasks exactly like you or, honestly, as well as you do, but that's ok! We still shouldn't attempt to carry our burdens alone. Grief is solitary, but care is communal. Let others know your needs and accept help from them.

*Lord, help me to lay down my pride and accept help.*

# 29

# GOD WILL PROVIDE

*"Go to the sea and cast a hook and take the first fish that comes up, and when you open its mouth you will find a shekel. Take that and give it to them for me and for yourself."*

MATTHEW 17:27 ESV

Around his first birthday, Lucas became attached to a particular sippy cup, and nineteen years later, he still demands this same cup model.

We have tried everything to get him to accept another drinking option, including therapy, straws, bribery (chocolate milk), allowing only water in the beloved cup of choice, but nothing has worked. In fact, I believe Lucas would rather wither away from dehydration than allow his lips to touch a drinking device that is not this cup.

You can imagine how distraught I became a few years ago when I discovered that the manufacturer of his favorite cup had discontinued this item. I desperately searched for the remaining products and found only a handful from places like eBay and secondhand stores. I did what any sane mother would do. I pleaded my case on Facebook.

I begged people far and wide to please help me find these sippy cups, and lo and behold, the solution came from the oddest place. An American woman living in Hong Kong emailed me with amazing news: "Jess! I found two hundred cups! All brand new! Where should I send them?"

God will provide for our needs, and often in ways we least expect it. It might be inside the mouth of a fish or from a woman living in Hong Kong. Ask with expectancy and faith, and then move out of God's way and watch him work.

*Father, thank you for your faithfulness in providing for all my needs.*

# 30

# GOOD GIFTS

*"Which of you, if your son asks for bread, will give him a stone? Or if he asks for a fish, will give him a snake? If you, then, though you are evil, know how to give good gifts to your children, how much more will your Father in heaven give good gifts to those who ask him!"*

MATTHEW 7:9–11 NIV

One morning, Ryan and I sipped our coffee and discussed the upcoming day, and I asked him a question that had become a regular inquiry after weeks of his insomnia: "How'd you sleep last night?"

I expected his same answer that I had received for weeks: "Not great." But instead, he surprised me.

"Actually, really well." he declared.

I asked what changed, and he explained, "I prayed, *Lord, please help me sleep*, and I did. I feel great!"

I laughed and thought, *Isn't it sad how often we forget to ask the Lord for what we need?*

Scripture specifically tells us that the Lord wants to give good gifts to his children, but there's a catch: we have to ask and be in a right relationship with him. There is movement in the spiritual realm when our faith meets action. The act of asking reveals a posture of submission and humility, a posture of surrender when we say, *Lord, I need you. Please help.*

What do you need to ask the Lord for today? Humble yourself and ask him. He is able and willing.

> *Lord, I ask you to please grant me the good gifts that I need, and I praise you for your faithfulness.*

# 31

# A MINISTRY OF CARE

*Whatever you do, work at it with all your heart,*
*as working for the Lord, not for human masters.*
COLOSSIANS 3:23 NIV

I recently experienced a day when I spun my wheels and felt like I didn't accomplish much real "work." But then I took inventory of my day. I got Lucas ready and put him on the bus. I did a load of his laundry. I prayed for my family, ordered Lucas's meds, washed the dishes, had a phone conversation with his caseworker, made a batch of banana bread (for him, hiding nutrition for the win!), ran errands—but managed to make it back home in time to get him off the bus after his caregiver canceled, and filled out paperwork I found in his backpack. I even walked two miles. Caregiver self-care is always a bonus!

Once I reflected on my day, I found I had actually accomplished a lot in my true ministry. I worked with all my heart, and in doing so, I worked for the Lord. I served in the ministry of care.

As caregivers, we should ask ourselves, *Is my caregiving a ministry from the Lord, and if so, what do I need to say no to in order to work effectively at this ministry with all my heart?* Maybe it's quitting a job outside the home or declining a volunteer position or opportunity. Maybe it's saying no to sports activities for a time.

In this spring season of finding a rhythm and a new normal, we will have to say no to good and worthy things so that we can say yes to the caregiving ministry that Jesus has called us to. And in that yes, we become testaments to the good news of God's grace.

*Lord, may I always work for you with all my heart and accomplish my duties.*

# 32

# MUNDANE OBEDIENCE

*"I ask you, LORD, please kill me.*
*It is better for me to die than to live."*
JONAH 4:3 NCV

W e are so often like Jonah, full of faith during the difficult
times, praising the Lord as the storms rage, raising our hands in
surrender, and bending our knees as we beg for reprieve. I was on
fire for the Lord when Lucas was diagnosed with a stroke in utero. I
sought out moments of desperate worship with my Savior because I
was desperate for hope.

Something about major trauma (or being swallowed by a
whale) quickly drops us to our knees, and we declare, *You are God,
and I am not. Thy will be done.* However, when the trauma passes
and the whale spits us out onto dry land, when we return to our
normal, everyday, boring life of making meals and washing clothes

and wiping bottoms and sitting beneath trees, we also often return to blah.

In that blah, maybe we don't literally wish to die (or maybe we do sometimes), but we feel less on fire, less faithful, less fervent, and less enthusiastic about our lives. In all actuality, though, the boring mundane is where faith meets obedience.

It's the everyday tasks that burn away impurities and chisel us. It's in the eye of the storm or in the belly of a whale where we acknowledge our Maker. But it's the tiresome, everyday obedience where we become like our Maker.

*Lord, help me to remember to be thankful when the pressures of life decrease and when life feels routine and mundane.*

# 33

# PURSUE THEIR HEARTS

*"Behold, I, I myself will search for my sheep
and will seek them out."*
EZEKIEL 34:11 ESV

I was chatting with a friend about some difficult behaviors that Lucas was exhibiting, and she described a similar experience she had with her daughter. She explained how she was crying out to the Lord, asking him to show her how to pursue her daughter's heart.

I paused and wrote the phrase "pursue her heart" on a tattered napkin. Maybe that was the key to overcoming my difficulties with Lucas. Maybe I wasn't pursuing his heart, and I wondered, *What would it look like if I did?*

That evening, as Lucas sat on the floor playing with his iPad, I joined him. Legs crisscross applesauce, I entered his space. I gently took his hands and began to play "pat-a-cake, pat-a-cake." His smile lit up the room, and his head swayed back and forth in delight. I pursued his heart, his way of seeing the world, and in turn, I entered his sacred space. I pursued him as the Lord pursues me when he joins me on my daily walks.

How can you pursue the hearts of your loved ones? Do you need to plop yourself on the floor with your child like I did? Or watch twenty reruns of the same show? Or maybe you need to accompany your loved one to a chemo treatment? Pursue their hearts as the Lord pursues yours.

*Thank you, Lord, for your constant pursuit of my heart.*

# 34

# THE LORD'S PRAYER

*Our Father which art in heaven,*
*hallowed be thy name.*
MATTHEW 6:9–13 KJV

Today's devotion deviates in structure from the rest of the devotions in this book. You see, one morning, I read the Lord's Prayer as if it were written specifically for me, a caregiver. After each verse, I paused to personalize my prayer in response. I encourage you, fellow caregiver, to try this same exercise.

Our Father which art in heaven, hallowed be thy name.

*Lord, I come before you, tired and overwhelmed. I acknowledge your headship over my life. I claim your sovereignty and ask that your name be glorified through my obedience.*

Thy kingdom come, thy will be done in earth,
as it is in heaven.

*I pray that through my obedience I may be a vessel that ushers in
your kingdom here on earth, a kingdom of love, joy, and peace, as
I serve the least of these. I pray that your will always takes priority
over my desires.*

Give us this day our daily bread.

*Supply my needs for only today. I pray that you multiply my sleep,
my loved one's sleep, my time, my energy, and my finances. I pray
for the emotional and physical strength to be a caregiver in this
moment and this moment alone.*

And forgive us our debts, as we forgive our debtors.

*Forgive me when I complain or serve with bitterness and help me
to forgive those who haven't helped. Thank you for your everlasting
forgiveness and love.*

And lead us not into temptation, but deliver us from evil:
For thine is the kingdom, and the power, and the glory, for ever.

*Keep me humble, Lord. May I not fall into the temptation of
victimhood or the desire for people to praise me for a job well
done. May my life always point people back to you, for everything
I am and all that I do is for your glory. You alone are worthy forever
and ever. Amen.*

# 35

# DOING WHAT WORKS

*"The Sabbath was made for man,*
*not man for the Sabbath."*

MARK 2:27 NIV

When we lived in rural Tennessee, we struggled to find a church that could accommodate Lucas's unique needs. Our never-ending search required us to visit a new church every week, and our kids would ask, "Can't we skip church today?" And on many Sundays, we would.

We'd toss our church clothes back into the closet and head to the park for a picnic. A park where the kids laughed, ran, and played. A park where Lucas was free to be himself, walking, playing, and shimmying down the slide, swaying his head in delight as he hollered, "Go whee!" A park where we watched in holy awe, marveling at the miracle of Lucas's life and thanking Jesus for his faithfulness.

I believe in the value of communal worship, but I also believe there are caregiving seasons when it isn't optimal. I look back on my season when Jason was fighting cancer, unable to orient himself at church. I would guide him and Lucas through the lobby while also pushing my son Joshua in a stroller as his brother, Caleb, tagged along behind, holding the hand of his sister, Mabel.

I arose each Sunday morning during that season because of my own expectation that I should go to church. But I wish I had given myself the grace to say *no*. Grace to admit to myself, *This doesn't work for our family right now.* I should have understood that the Sabbath was made for me and my need for rest, not the other way around.

What expectation from others or yourself do you need to release to find the rest you need?

*Lord, help me release the expectations of others and myself to do what you call me to do.*

# 36

# FIND YOUR COMMUNITY

*If either of them falls down, one can help the other up.*
*But pity anyone who falls and has no one to help them up.*
ECCLESIASTES 4:10 NIV

I once had an extremely busy weekend ahead of me that included two speaking events and a book signing. On top of all that, Ryan was out of town for work, which meant I was parenting solo that weekend too. Ryan rarely had to travel once we moved to my home state of Michigan, but when we lived in Tennessee, his traveling was a regular occurrence.

My anxiety would rise days before he left because we had so few people we could rely on for help. It was a big reason behind our return to Michigan in the first place. We were so desperate for support that we traded in sunshine, sweet tea, and isolation for snow shovels, breweries, and community.

My family and friends in Michigan came through while Ryan was away that busy weekend. While I was in the middle of preparing dinner, reviewing my speech notes, and frantically applying makeup, my friend sent me a text: "How can I help?"

Normally, I would have responded with a fake, cheery disposition: "I'm fine, but thanks!" followed by several happy emojis, but this time I didn't. I was truthful and accepted my friend's help. She stepped into the chaos with me (and boy, was it chaotic), and it was a blessing to feel seen, loved, and supported.

Many caregivers find their communities online, and yes, it is a valuable form of community. Still, nothing can replace people in the flesh stepping in and helping when you need it. Find these people in this season of caregiving. Pursue your people. We were made for real-life community.

*Father, help me to take tangible steps toward finding a real-life community.*

# 37

# PLANS OR PURPOSE

*Many are the plans in a person's heart
but it is the LORD's purpose that prevails.*
PROVERBS 19:21 NIV

One summer, I planned for Lucas to be in school so that I could write this devotional, but then his school district decreased his hours, which meant he wouldn't attend a full school day. I had my plan all worked out, and now my dreams were going to have to take a back seat, once again, to my caregiving duties.

I was angry, and that anger morphed into bitterness. I stewed for a bit before realizing that holding on to bitterness was simply a waste of my energy. I made a choice to change my narrative from victim to victor.

I knew it was God's purpose that I write this book, and I also knew it was God's purpose that I care for my son. The two didn't align. I was called to both, and I had to have faith that God would provide. If he brought me to it, he would see me through it.

I prayed for restful sleep and that the Lord would supernaturally multiply my time. Of course, I also had to take action to make these things happen. I went to bed on time and woke up early to write. This simple habit led to good sleep, which multiplied my time and culminated in the completion of this book. The Lord, in his great provision, also brought help in the form of a local high school student who offered to care for Lucas a few days a week.

What plans of yours aren't working out exactly as you anticipated? Make sure you obey his will and believe his purpose will prevail. Then take action to make it happen.

*Lord, help me focus on your purpose in my life.*

# 38

# IN REMEMBRANCE OF ME

*He took bread, gave thanks and broke it, and gave it to them, saying,*
*"This is my body given for you; do this in remembrance of me."*
LUKE 22:19 NIV

I descended the stairs, irritated by what was awaiting me on this Good Friday. Lucas required another diaper change, a chore that lately was able to grate my very last nerve. I did what was necessary, and he began to sing in his sweet, jumbled way. He repeated the words until I joined, which I did, although a little unwillingly because the smell still lingered in the air.

People often found Jesus among the Lucases of the world, serving in whatever capacity their needs required. Jesus would have changed Lucas's diaper with joy. And on Good Friday, a day when caregivers walk the *Via Dolorosa*, "the way of grief," as the air is thick with despair, our souls scream in quiet desperation, *It is finished! We are finished!* And yes, life as we know it is finished;

it will never be the same. But we hold on with every ounce of strength that remains within our weary souls because life is always intertwined with death. Resurrection Sunday is around the bend.

And until then? We remember the holy, mundane tasks—*do this in remembrance of me*—the bread and the wine, the body broken and the blood spilled for us. And may our remembrance lead to an ongoing resurrection as we serve in uncomfortable spaces holding unpleasant smells and as we wash feet and change diapers if need be.

May we serve in these reverent places of vulnerability and in the long silences as we tend to the needs of others—the holiest of work as we care for the least of these.

*Lord, grant me a resurrected perspective and a holy shift in attitude.*

**39**

# TRUST ONLY GOD

*Jesus did not commit himself unto them...*
*for he knew what was in man.*
JOHN 2:24–25 KJV

Jesus trusted *only* his heavenly Father. He placed his trust in no one else and was able to successfully complete his earthly mission because he never took his eyes off his Father's will.

Sometimes it's easy to focus on the people or systems or government programs that aren't addressing our needs or helping us in our struggles. Sometimes it's easy to make up our own stories as to why they don't help, and then we fixate on those imaginary stories. Sometimes it's easy to become bitter and resentful. I've been there.

I became bitter and resentful when we lived in Tennessee. I met with every person I could find who held authority within the complex disability system, and every meeting ended with, "We're sorry. There are no services, no homes, no help, no waiver funds, no respite, nothing." And I took that to mean that no one cared, but this wasn't the case.

I had a heavenly Father who cared deeply, and when I prayed about his will for our lives, doors opened for us to return to Michigan. We trusted his will and did not focus on what couldn't be done. Instead, we fixed our gaze on what he had called us to do.

We walk a fine line as caregivers, and we might carry an expectation that the government or the systems that we citizens have put in place to help *will* actually help. But Jesus committed himself entirely to his Father's will and placed his trust in what he was able to accomplish through him, not in what man could or could not do.

*Jesus, I place my trust in you alone.*

# 40

# FINDING BEAUTY

*To appoint unto them that mourn in Zion, to give unto them beauty for ashes, the oil of joy for mourning, the garment of praise for the spirit of heaviness; that they might be called trees of righteousness, the planting of the LORD, that He might be glorified.*

ISAIAH 61:3 KJV

One spring afternoon, we brought Lucas to a respite program for individuals with disabilities. The plan (don't we love the plans we make!) was to enjoy a few hours of fun with our other kids. The program was a forty-five-minute drive, and as we drove, the kids became restless, which led to arguing and bickering and to Lucas stimming and screaming. And so, I did what any mom would do and had a come-to-Jesus moment.

I informed my children that I would not reward bad behavior. I told them if I didn't see improvement by the time we arrived, we would cancel all the fun (and then I desperately prayed that they would pull it together so that we wouldn't have to actually cancel the fun).

One smart-alecky child decided to push their luck and got snarky. I replied with "the look" and the question, "Are you seriously back talking right now? I believe the response you're after is, 'Yes, Mom.'"

Then Lucas, who had been quiet during my impassioned speech, yelled out, "Yes, Mom!"

I cried tears of joy because that was the first time my boy had ever called me "Mom."

It's easy to get so caught up in the difficulties of life that we forget to appreciate the beauty. What small victories can you be thankful for today?

*Thank you, Jesus, for snarky attitudes that lead to answered prayers.*

# 41

# PRAYER CHANGES CIRCUMSTANCES

*The LORD turned the captivity of Job,*
*when he prayed for his friends.*
JOB 42:10 KJV

I often find it's easier to stay home rather than navigate the complexities of the outside world with Lucas. And this isolated existence, when compounded by a lack of support, can feel like a prison.

This feeling of isolation was at its worst in 2020, given the worldwide pandemic. It proved an extremely challenging period. I didn't have the capacity to do much, but I did have time to pray. I prayed for breakthroughs and solutions. I prayed for peace and rest, and I prayed that Lucas would somehow understand why he couldn't attend school (or, at the very least, that he would accept his lot in life).

Although my prayers didn't make the pandemic magically go away, they did bring peace. We settled into a "new normal" and received answers through medication that we had been reluctant for Lucas to try. We saw a major reduction in his anxiety, which led to more verbal output from him and less screaming.

God used our period of captivity to open our minds to try anything, and that anything led to a surprising treatment that has proved to be a game changer for our son and for us, his caregivers.

If you feel like you're in a period of captivity, remember that you have all the time in the world to pray. Pray for your loved one, yourself, and others, and watch as God opens doors and releases chains of bondage.

*Lord, help me to remember to use my time of captivity to pray for others.*

# 42

# IMAGE BEARERS

*God created mankind in his own image,*
*in the image of God he created them;*
*male and female, he created them.*

GENESIS 1:27 NIV

Lately I've tried to reframe my focus to see the image of God in every single person I encounter: the guy who cuts me off in traffic, the troll on the internet who called me horrible names, and the acquaintance who backstabbed me.

As I've focused on truly seeing each person as an image bearer of the Lord, I've found that, at times, it's the most difficult to give the same grace to those who are constantly present in my life—my husband, Lucas, and our other children. We work out many of our issues on those we love the most because we know they are safe and will still love and tolerate us.

It's difficult to see the image of God in Lucas when he's screaming or smearing his food all over the wall or yanking my arm in frustration, but just because it's hard to see doesn't mean it's not the reality; Lucas was created in the image of God, just as I was or anyone else for that matter. He bears the stamp of the Almighty: in his disability, in his behaviors, and in his frustration. I'm definitely a work in progress, and I continue to try.

Are you able to see those people in your life as image bearers of God? How about your loved one for whom you are a caregiver? Has it become more difficult to see the image of God in them since the diagnosis or disability? Or has it become easier? Think about this and then resolve to see each person you encounter as a unique creation bearing the stamp of God.

*Lord, may I see and truly understand that everyone is created in your image.*

# 43

# COME OUT OF HIDING

The LORD God called out to the man, "Where are you?"
"I heard Your voice in the garden," he replied,
"and I was afraid because I was naked; so I hid myself."
GENESIS 3:9–10 BSB

Our family was invited to an ice cream social at our daughter's school one spring. Normally we would have found someone to watch Lucas while we took the other children because he can be extremely messy with ice cream (it's a sensory issue) and pretty vocal with crowds (another sensory issue), and he doesn't care at all about how his actions make others feel (his mother's sensory issue).

But I was over it. I was done feeling shame and embarrassment about how others would perceive his actions or oddities, and I was ready to show the world my reality, to show a tiny glimpse of my caregiving journey. We left the comfort of our home and ventured out.

When we all arrived at the ice cream social, we sat on the outskirts of the playground because Lucas was shouting, "All done!" as soon as we arrived. We fed him ice cream, and he removed every bite from his mouth to examine it before putting it back in.

A few brave souls said hello, and one of those individuals asked if she could help. We had exposed ourselves. We exposed our life and came out of hiding and entered an uncomfortable, exhausting, and anxious situation because it was time for the world to see families like mine. It was time for us to enter our community.

*Lord, help me to remember to be a part of the community, even if it's difficult at times.*

# 44

# GLORY TO GOD

*"This happened so that the works of God
might be displayed in his life."*
JOHN 9:3 NIV

Lucas lives in Lucas's world. He has no pretensions or ulterior motives and is happy with *Veggie Tales*, food, a clean diaper, and chocolate milk. He has taught me so much about our human ideas of perfection and the standards people have for each other because Lucas is exactly how God intended him to be. He is a beautiful testimony of God's faithfulness, and he's touched many lives through his perceived imperfections.

Many have questioned the purpose of Lucas's life or quoted the verse, "Who sinned, this man or his parents, that he was born blind?" (John 9:2), and the answer is exactly as Christ proclaims, "This happened so that the works of God might be displayed in him" (v. 3). He has not been healed to the extent that my limited imagination envisioned during my pregnancy with him, but over the years, he has healed me and many others of misconceptions we hold regarding healing and our God.

We possess such a narrow understanding of the words *healing* and *healed*. Lucas is perfect the way God created him. His very existence screams glory to God, and that is the point of our lives. To bring glory to our Father in heaven through our faithful obedience to whatever trials he calls us to endure, whether that be as a person with a disability or as a caregiver.

*Lord, may my faithful obedience glorify you.*

# 45

# DISCERNMENT

*Do not be conformed to this world, but be transformed by the renewal of your mind, that by testing you may discern what is the will of God, what is good and acceptable and perfect.*

ROMANS 12:2 ESV

The gift of trauma unearths in us a distinct laser-sharp focus that crystalizes over time. What once was difficult to see or understand, such as ideas, decisions, and relationships, becomes clear as we take one labored step after another alongside our loved ones. The beauty of this hardship is that it helps us determine what should remain and what we must release.

I recently grasped this truth when my girlfriends asked me to run away with them for a fun weekend and I had to say no. There are exciting, life-giving events and activities that I simply cannot commit to because I am a caregiver.

I have to say *no* because I discerned the will of the Father when I said *yes* to Lucas. For years, this realization stung, and then, somewhere along the path, I made peace with it. Perhaps the peace occurred when I understood that my work was holy. Or maybe it shifted once we had a plan in place for Lucas's future.

But part of this focus required me to discern who and what activities had my best interest at heart versus those that did not. I had to pay attention to who was watching, waiting, and maybe curious about my life but not invested. Then I had to release those individuals to make way for the beauty that arrived through others who *did* care. I had to release those activities that did not serve me so that I could accomplish the will of God, which is perfect.

*Father, grant me a refined focus for what must stay*
*and what must go.*

# 46

# THE GIFT OF CAREGIVING

*In order to keep me from becoming conceited,*
*I was given a thorn in my flesh.*
2 CORINTHIANS 12:7 NIV

We each have the potential to perceive ourselves as better than we are. I could easily delight in how special I think I am and lean into pride and its enticing offers. I think about this within the realm of my creative endeavors, projects that could potentially cast a bright light on me and thrust me into a world for which I am unprepared. And yet…

I will continue to rise every morning
and care for my disabled son
and bathe him
and help him get dressed
and pour juice into his sippy cup
and put socks upon his feet

and lace up his sneakers
and hold his hand as we walk down the driveway together.

This is my routine every single day. Like the apostle Paul, my actions, though monotonous, serve as my own prickly thorn, breathing humility into my swelling soul and deflating any pride that tries to sneak in.

This uncomfortable road, this thorn of caregiving, this aching joy is a gift, a gift that calls me to lay down my life and reminds me of who I am and who I am not by stripping away any pretenses. In the presence of fame, fortune, and pride, this gift keeps me grounded and prepares a table before me, where I dine in the community of caregivers, feasting on humility and gulping down goblets of grace.

It is well with my soul. It is well with Lucas's soul. And that is enough.

*Lord, keep me humble and use whatever means*
*necessary for me to give you the glory and praise.*

# 47

# TEAMWORK

*Bear one another's burdens,*
*and so fulfill the law of Christ.*

GALATIANS 6:2 NKJV

We've encountered a lot of concern about Lucas's siblings throughout the years—well-meaning concern but misdirected. The concern originates from the idea that the siblings of a disabled child don't receive enough time or attention from us because we are too busy with Lucas's needs. There's an element of truth here, as Lucas is profoundly disabled and requires more hands-on care than our other children do.

However, Ryan and I encourage a philosophy of teamwork within our family structure. And on our team, we have a member who requires more help. Therefore, in obedience to Christ's commandment to "bear one another's burdens," we all help out.

This structure trickles into many aspects of our family life. We each help with Lucas, we collectively enjoy family kickball games—including Lucas who is pushed in his stroller as he rounds the bases, and we all sit down at the dinner table at night and enjoy a meal together.

In cultivating our family team, we cultivate the love of Christ, who was almost always among a group or a team of disciples or working his way through a community. God created us to do life together, and in this way, we fulfill the law of Christ.

Do you feel guilty that you don't have the same amount of time for others that you had before you became a caregiver? Take heart. Christ calls us to bear one another's burdens.

*Lord, thank you for those who help me bear my burdens.*

# 48

# FRESH JOY

*The humble will be filled with fresh joy from the LORD.*
ISAIAH 29:19 NLT

Lucas has this new thing that he does every night. Around 8 p.m., he slowly emerges from his tattered, brown leather chair, drops his beloved iPad, searches for Dad, grabs his hand, and says, "Gotabeh (go to bed)." Dad takes him to bed, tucks him in, and says, "I love you," and Lucas responds, "I wuv you."

We went fifteen years without a single word, and now our son speaks sentences. If that doesn't fall under the category of "fresh joy," then I don't know what does.

Isn't it amazing how God loves us so much that he blesses us with seemingly insignificant moments of joy—insignificant in the eyes of the world but overflowing with significance in our caregiver eyes?

For us, these joyful moments often arrive in Lucas learning how to speak. Will he ever be fully verbal? I don't know, but these glimpses of fresh joy fill me with hope that one day, when he is made whole in eternity, my son will be completely able to articulate his thoughts—when we are all made whole. Some of us simply have more noticeable challenges and disabilities than others.

What fresh joy are you currently experiencing in this season? Is your father in remission? Or maybe your daughter has been sleeping through the night. Allow these moments to permeate your soul as you bask in the wonder of our God's goodness. Allow this joy to strengthen and sustain not only your caregiving journey but also your walk with the Lord.

*Thank you, Jesus, for filling me with fresh joy.*

# 49

# BLESSED ARE YOU

*"Blessed are the poor in spirit."*
MATTHEW 5:3 NIV

Blessed are the poor in spirit and those who humbly spend their days caring for others. Blessed are those who go unnoticed as they rise at the crack of dawn to replenish meds or empty catheter bags. Blessed are those who insert life-sustaining needles into weary veins and hold the hands of those who are not long for this world.

Blessed are those who gently slip arms into sleeves and pull pants upon limp limbs. Blessed are those who feed and bathe and assist their loved ones in getting from one place to another. Blessed are those who sacrifice for the kingdom in isolated and unrecognized spaces. Blessed are those who do not strive for beauty, glamor, or popularity or clamor for the things of this world.

Blessed are those who influence the lives of the poorest in spirit, those whose patience runs thin, or those whose bottoms we wipe. Blessed are those whose bodies have betrayed them, forcing them now to rely on others. Blessed are those whose cells are ravaged by chemo and radiation. Blessed are those who can't remember our names.

Blessed are all of them and blessed are we for entering the fellowship of suffering, entering exhaustive, isolating, and lonely spaces, and entering the depravity of the poor in spirit because it is through our affliction that we usher in the kingdom of heaven to a weary world.

*Father, thank you for my poverty of spirit as a caregiver because, in my poverty, I am blessed.*

# 50

# IN ALL THINGS GIVE THANKS

*In everything give thanks;*
*for this is the will of God for you in Christ Jesus.*

1 THESSALONIANS 5:18 NASB

Goodness gracious, it sure can be difficult to find things to be thankful for as a caregiver when dealing with autism, diabetes, Alzheimer's, cancer, and other diagnoses and disabilities. It's not easy to praise the Lord for aggressive, repetitive behaviors, diaper changes, forgotten memories, and post-treatment vomiting.

I remember when Jason and I ventured out for our anniversary only months before he passed away. The treatments had made him so sick that our date ended in the emergency room. I was not feeling thankful at that point. And honestly, we don't necessarily have to be thankful for these hard moments. But we can and should find something that we are thankful for.

Instead of dwelling on the unfairness that our anniversary ended in the ER, I could have concentrated on how grateful I was to celebrate ten years with my husband. I could have appreciated the blessings of my children or the community that surrounded us as we walked through a deep, dark valley.

It's easier to find joy when we focus on the beauty instead of the ashes. Do you have a home? A loving spouse? Food? Friends and family? As you enter the summer season and the heat begins to rise, shift your focus to the positives. God will replace your spirit of heaviness with joy and praise.

*Father, I thank you for the everyday blessings that I often take for granted.*

# SUMMER

*Day and night your hand was heavy upon me;*
*my strength was dried up as by the heat of summer.*
PSALM 32:4 ESV

We've entered summer, when caregiving feels hot and heavy. We plead for a miracle because the treatments have stopped working, or perhaps our child is experiencing new medical problems, or our loved one has relapsed, or maybe our son or daughter has entered puberty, and their aggression and destructive behaviors have grown intense.

We've grown weary of the never-ending duties, and our lives begin to feel overwhelmingly difficult. We find ourselves trapped in a loop of distress, lacking any sort of rhythm or routine.

Summer is a season of exhaustion and deep grief, as we once again face our caregiving reality, which feels oppressive and unfair. Yet we hold on to he who is greater than he who is in the world (1 John 4:4). Because it is in him where we find our solace and strength.

# 51

# NEW MERCIES

*Great is his faithfulness;*
*his mercies begin afresh each morning.*

LAMENTATIONS 3:23 NLT

One beautiful summer day, I took my children to the park. The kids excitedly ran off to play, and I encouraged Lucas to join. "Come on, Lucas!" I coaxed. But he screamed and reached to pull my hair. "Lucas, let's play!" I tried again.

Lucas continued to scream and started to circle the van, pacing around it like a tiger trapped inside a cage, except Lucas wanted to go back inside the van. He tried each window before yanking on the door handles, the windshield wipers, and then my body.

A nearby father grabbed his young son's hand and walked away from the disturbance. "Lucas Aaron," I hissed, "do not ruin this for everyone!"

Instead, Lucas pulled me down onto the hot asphalt with him. We sat there together while he screamed and stimmed, only wanting what made sense to him: to return home to his favorite brown chair and his favorite iPad with its blue case. He wanted only that and nothing else. I sat beside him, fighting back tears. I remembered my once sweet little boy who was now an aggressive teenager and not so sweet if truth be told. I contemplated his future, our future, and then I rose.

"Alright, you win," I whispered and opened the van door, admitting defeat only ten minutes after arriving at the park. I hollered to my other children, "Sorry, kids, Lucas is done. Time to go home. We'll try again tomorrow."

Tomorrow we will rise again and face a new day. We hope for a better outcome. We pray for answers and maybe one tiny win because God's mercies are new every morning.

*Father, thank you for fresh mercy.*

# 52

# FRUIT

*The fruit of the Spirit is love, joy, peace, forbearance,
kindness, goodness, faithfulness, gentleness and self-control.
Against such things there is no law.*

GALATIANS 5:22–23 NIV

I got Lucas on the bus one rainy morning, a tedious task as I helped him ambulate. I pulled our minivan up over the sidewalk to avoid the rain, and as I walked him up the bus stairs, a woman rode by on her bike and yelled, "Hey! This is the bike path! Cars don't belong on it!"

I so badly wanted to rip into her and give her a piece of my mind and tell her what a rotten, no-good human being she was for failing to recognize and understand that I was helping my profoundly disabled son. I had a slew of choice words ready to unleash.

But the Spirit said, *Stop. Display fruit.*

*No!* my flesh cried. *That woman deserves my spiteful barrage of words!*

And I heard it again. *Those who belong to me display patience, love, joy, peace, forbearance, kindness, goodness, faithfulness, gentleness, and self-control.*

My perfectly appropriate (yet slightly sinful) barrage of words would have pretty much canceled out every single fruit. Instead, I surrendered and practiced self-control. *One out of nine ain't bad,* I thought.

It's easy to justify our bad behavior because of our difficult lives, but regardless of our circumstances, fruit is the measure of the One we belong to. What fruit are you displaying in your life, and where can you do better?

*Lord, help me to display the fruit even when my flesh wants to do anything but display fruit.*

## 53

# You Did It for Me

*"The King will answer them, 'Truly, I say to you, as you did it to one of the least of these my brothers, you did it to me.'"*

Matthew 25:40 ESV

*This is holy work*, I begrudgingly reminded myself after returning home from a much-needed vacation. After a week of sun, relaxation, and time reconnecting with Ryan, there I was again, changing Lucas's diaper. It was his third bout of diarrhea that month. So many wipes. So many diapers. So many hand washes and missed school days.

My frustration mounted with each smelly task added to my daily to-do list, a long list written prior to vacation that had doubled after returning home, especially with my career as an executive director of a nonprofit pushing forward. Exciting developments were on the horizon! God-ordained news!

But this moment? This smelly moment? A moment I couldn't have dreamed about in 2004 after Lucas's dismal prognosis when words like *terminate* hung in the air? A moment laden in God's plan? *Yes,* I sighed in surrender.

This mundane, underwhelming moment wasn't remotely exciting or glamorous. It wasn't Lights! Camera! Action! No contracts or meetings with important people. No, it matched none of those high and mighty ambitions or anything, really, that anyone in their right mind would strive to accomplish on a regular basis if given the choice.

It was a simple, humble moment that fell under holy obedience—humility-building holy, swallow-your-big-honkin'-ball-of-pride holy. Whatever-you-do-to-the-least-of-these type of holy. Dutifully performing—against every natural desire—what God had called me to do.

Every action or inaction is part of a grander plan, a plan that requires a holy obedience to God's eternal will.

*Father, may I always serve the least of these as if I were serving you.*

# 54

# HE WILL NOT FORSAKE YOU

*The LORD loves the just*
*and will not forsake his faithful ones.*

PSALM 37:28 NIV

T he day began rough, that summer day in 2009, when I awoke at 2 a.m. to Jason making pancakes. Brain cancer had eaten away his sensibilities, and he believed morning had arrived. He thought he was being helpful by cooking breakfast for our family.

I remember feeling a depth of despair that I had not yet felt up until that day. I truly felt like God had forgotten and forsaken me. I was overwhelmingly exhausted, and now I had to care for my husband in the middle of the night, and I would have to care for my four young children throughout the day.

I helped Jason back into bed and wept, deep wells of grief spilling out in the early morning hours. In my despair, the Lord reminded me, *I am here. I am present. I will not leave you or forsake you, but you must surrender to my care.* You'll notice a consistent theme with me and the Lord. Surrender is apparently a lesson I don't learn easily.

I surrendered again on that painful day, and in my surrender, a woman from Caleb's school called and offered to watch my children and my husband so that I could take a nap. The Lord was there all along.

*Thank you, Lord, for never leaving us or forsaking us.*

55

# SURRENDER

*Jesus said to His disciples, "If anyone wants to come after Me,*
*he must deny himself, take up his cross, and follow Me."*
MATTHEW 16:24 NASB

I give you everything!" I sang along with a song, belting out this sentiment, and the Lord whispered to me, *Will you give me everything?*

*Yes, Lord!* I agreed, but the nudging continued.

*What about that thing that helps you cope? That thing you turn to for peace instead of turning to me?*

*Lord,* I explained, *I need that thing! This caregiving season is so difficult. I deserve that thing!*

And the Lord said, *Then no, you have not given me everything. You have not completely surrendered your life because you cling to this thing and worship this thing instead of denying yourself to follow me.*

After weeks of conviction, I reluctantly laid the thing down. I admitted my helplessness and surrendered, and within a week, I saw movement in the spiritual realm after having been stuck for years. I witnessed breakthroughs in my children, in my marriage, and in my son, who had been so incredibly difficult to that point. In my lack of surrender, I held captive supernatural movement, and in my surrender, a spiritual shift occurred.

Most of us have that precious thing that helps us cope in our hours of desperation. And when that thing becomes our heart, it becomes our idol. What is your thing? Where do you invest time and treasure? Maybe it's shopping, scrolling social media, gambling, gossiping, or abusing alcohol or drugs. Whatever it may be, will you give it to the Lord today?

*Father, I surrender. I give you everything because
I trust that your best for my life will come as I
release control.*

# 56

# GIVING AND RECEIVING CARE

*"This is what the Sovereign LORD says: Woe to you shepherds of Israel who only take care of yourselves! Should not shepherds take care of the flock?"*

EZEKIEL 34:2 NIV

Whenever I start to feel sorry for myself and what I've been called to endure, a good ole romp through the Old Testament shifts my perspective pretty quickly. What some of these Old Testament prophets were called to endure for the sake of "God's chosen people" is far beyond my sacrificial abilities.

Still, throughout Scripture, we find the call to care for each other and to care for the flock we've been given. From Genesis to Revelation, this obedience to caring for one another is what pleases the Lord.

Humanity used to operate more like tribes, seeing and helping its vulnerable members. We've wandered far away from this model, hiding away those who need care the most. Now our society is experiencing detrimental consequences—astronomical rates of anxiety, depression, and suicide—because of our lack of care.

The bookends of this life journey involve giving and receiving care. It's a part of the arch of the human experience. We enter the world needing care, and we will likely leave the world requiring it too. We're fortunate if we don't require it in between.

Caregivers, when you feel disheartened and unable to continue, remember that you are part of the never-ending circle of care that God entrusted to humanity since the beginning of time. The Lord is pleased with those who care for his flock.

*Father, may I remember that my caring for others*
*pleases you.*

# 57

# PAPA'S DELIGHT

The LORD said to Satan, "Have you considered my servant Job?
There is no one on earth like him; he is blameless and upright,
a man who fears God and shuns evil."

JOB 1:8 NIV

On really tough caregiving days, I often replace Job's name with mine in this heavenly exchange between God and Satan: *Have you considered my servant Jess? She is (somewhat) blameless and upright, a woman who fears God and shuns evil. She will be faithful.*

This imaginary exchange brings me hope and encourages me in my weary situation. It reminds me that God sees each of us in our personal struggles. He saw Job and his faithfulness, and I trust that he sees me and my obedience as well.

Also noteworthy is God's bragging about Job. He's a proud Papa who is eager to share about his son. That's a nice thought: my heavenly Father bragging about me and finding delight in what I accomplish here on earth. And these thoughts inspire me to continuously serve my son in sacred spaces of caregiving, even when it's difficult.

What a gift to have our Papa bragging about our faithfulness! I have faith that I will one day be the recipient of this coveted bragging when I step into eternity and hear, *Well done, my good and faithful servant.* I have faith that you, too, will hear these words as you obediently fulfill God's purpose in your life.

*Father, may I compel you to delight in my obedience.*

58

# BELIEVE

*Stop doubting and believe.*
JOHN 20:27 NIV

When Lucas was seventeen, he lashed out almost daily, and I wondered how much longer I'd possess the physical strength to care for him. After sending him off to school for the day, I would often take a walk and wonder, *How do I continue to care for someone who has the potential to hurt me? What does our future look like? What are our options if no programs or housing options for disabled adults are available?*

Then my tears would flow because this was my baby boy, the child whom I was told would never live, and my deep desire to keep him safe had been replaced with despair and doubt. I recalled a favorite saying, spoken by Victor Raymond Edman, former president of Wheaton College, "Never doubt in the darkness what God has made clear in the light."[3]

I always had faith that God would provide. I always had faith that there would be a safe place for Lucas when the time arrived to release him into the world. But as Lucas grew older, my faith sounded more like that of a Doubting Thomas.

The Holy Spirit whispered, *Dear faithful Mama, place your hand in my side. Feel the agony I suffered at Calvary. Know how much I love you and Lucas. I will care for him. I will care for you, and I will provide in due time. In my time. My grace is sufficient for this moment. Simply move forward in obedience.*

Are you doubting a word that the Lord gave you in the light? Remember, he is faithful, and he will see his word come to pass.

*Lord, help my unbelief. I choose to trust your word.*

3  Dr. Wallace Alcorn, "Every Saying Has a Beginning, and Some Never End," Wheaton College, Alumni blog, November 11, 2016, https://www.wheaton.edu.

# 59

# RESTRAINT

*"Don't waste what is holy on people who are unholy.*
*Don't throw your pearls to pigs!*
*They will trample the pearls,*
*then turn and attack you."*

MATTHEW 7:6 NLT

Sometimes the temptation arises to moan and groan about how difficult our lives are. This moaning and groaning can solicit lots of sympathetic attention, which is comforting and validating when we're going through a difficult time.

People, by nature, are attracted to messy situations. We slow down when we see an accident on the side of the road, or we lean in to listen closely to a friend opening up about their divorce. The old adage "Misery loves company" is especially true in the caregiving world.

However, we must remember to practice restraint when we share information about our personal lives with others. Our moments of frailty, despair, and sadness are also hard and holy moments of reverence with our loved ones. We need to guard these moments carefully, as they are sacred pearls not to be thrown to pigs.

Many people in the world cannot understand our hearts as caregivers, and they don't want to either. Yes, of course, we need people we can honestly open up to, but we shouldn't give the whole world access to the intimate spaces that hold our pain and struggles.

Find a trusted friend and invite them into your sorrow and into your difficult moments. Allow them to comfort you. Allow the Lord to use your companions to minister to your weary heart. But remember the dignity of your loved one.

If you share, share with a softened lens, not bestowing the hard and holy details upon a world that does not and will not honor your journey.

*Lord, help me to always remember the dignity of my loved one and to honor the moments I spend caring for them.*

## 60

# LOVE YOUR ENEMIES

*"I tell you, love your enemies
and pray for those who persecute you."*

MATTHEW 5:44 NIV

I stared at the message, shocked at what it said. It was from a fellow caregiving mother, and she was upset. So upset that she used many choice words to describe me and, in her opinion, my inaction and apathy toward her situation and her child.

In full caregiver-advocacy mode, I was raising awareness and providing solutions, but because of her particular circumstances, our solution wasn't a suitable fit. For the welfare and safety of our other participants, we had to make difficult decisions.

I ached for her and felt her desperation. In many ways, I *was* her, which is why her words pierced me. And honestly, they ticked me off! I wanted to post her message on social media to show people what I deal with.

But as I contemplated my next move, the Spirit whispered, *Pray for her.*

*But Lord!* I wailed. *Did you see what she wrote?*

And the whisper continued, *Pray.*

So I prayed. I prayed that the Lord would give her strength, wisdom, and patience. I prayed that she would find the right resource for her child, and I prayed that I would be able to quickly forgive her.

Whom do you need to pray for today? Has someone wronged you in some way? Maybe abandoned you or misunderstood something about your caregiving journey? Pray for those who might not understand and pray for those who do not help you.

*Lord, I lay before you those who have hurt me.*
*May I love them as you have loved me.*

# 61

# LIVE FOR THE LORD

*LORD, I know that people's lives are not their own;*
*it is not for them to direct their steps.*
JEREMIAH 10:23 NIV

Smack dab in the middle of summer break, Lucas screams from the family room. He is dysregulated with his new on-again, off-again summer school schedule. His siblings are off playing in the neighborhood, and I am attempting to meet a deadline, which is becoming increasingly difficult with the constant screams from the basement.

Lucas wants someone to sit beside him. He wants a companion, and I want to finish writing my book. Lucas is not going to allow me to accomplish what I want to accomplish, and so I reluctantly give in. I surrender, not very joyfully, but I recognize that my life is not my own, and it is not for me to direct my steps.

I slowly descend to the basement, where he eagerly awaits my arrival. My presence calms him. I sit beside him, and we settle in with our devices, him on his iPad and me on my laptop, hoping to type a few more words before the end of the day.

I've said it before, and I'll say it again because the lesson is crucial: a spiritual shift occurs when we surrender. I was prepared to surrender my will for my day, and in that movement, there was blessing for me and for my son. I was able to complete my work and remain faithful to my caregiving call.

*Lord, may we recognize that our lives are not our*
*own and that it is you who directs our steps.*

# 62

# RELEASE STRESS

*Whenever the evil spirit from God bothered Saul,*
*David would play his harp.*
*Saul would relax and feel better,*
*and the evil spirit would go away.*

1 SAMUEL 16:23 CEV

W e were four weeks into a long stretch of a hospital stay after Lucas was admitted to the ICU. He'd suffered a shunt malfunction and infection in which cerebral spinal fluid became trapped in his body. It left him so lethargic and lifeless that he was unable to eat or stay awake.

Ryan and I were exhausted. We were caring both for our sick child and our healthy children, leaving us with very little time to care for ourselves. The constant aching in my joints told me that my body was keeping score, holding on to the trauma. I needed to release it somehow.

I also knew my children were feeling the stress, and collectively, as a family, we needed a solution. I purchased a disco ball and transformed our basement into a dance club. Every night after I returned from the hospital, we turned off the lights, turned on the disco ball, blasted music, and danced. Some of us enjoyed it more than others, but we all got our bodies moving. We shook off the stress and released the anxiety.

If stress becomes embedded in us, like it did with King Saul, it can manifest as evil. Our bodies break down, and our spirits wane. That's why we have to prioritize releasing our stress. Consider lions or tigers. After catching prey, they instinctively know to shake off the stress. As humans, we don't seem to know this or accept it as truth.

Set aside time to shake off your stress. Turn on some music, go for a walk, or watch a workout video while your loved one sleeps. The Lord desires that we care for ourselves.

*Lord, I commit to caring for my body and releasing*
*my stress.*

# 63

# WAIT

*Be still in the presence of the LORD,*
*and wait patiently for him to act.*
PSALM 37:7 NLT

W ait. We encounter this pesky little word often. Wait for a diagnosis, wait for a treatment protocol, wait for biopsy results, wait for healing, wait for a placement, wait for services, and, sometimes, wait for death.

Most of my grief over Lucas throughout the years had nothing to do with his diagnosis but with the uncertainty of his future and ours. This grief is directly tied to my lack of control over the situation and my inability to wait for the Lord's help. Waiting is hard when it comes to our loved ones because we desperately want to fix the situation—now.

Lisa Whittle says, "Immediate obedience is the instant yes to Jesus, no matter what. Long obedience is the enduring yes to

Jesus, no matter what."[4] I gave my immediate obedience when I chose life for Lucas, and I have displayed my obedience for more than nineteen years as I've continued to care for him.

As I waited for the Lord to rescue me, I had no idea if that rescue would come on this side of eternity or in heaven. I didn't know if we would find a home or someone to care for him or if his siblings would have to help or if he and I would cling to one another into old age. Then the Lord opened a door, and we purchased Hope Farm, which we turned into a group home for disabled adults.

We are called to be still (so hard!) and to wait patiently (even harder!) for God to act, and in that waiting in stillness and patience, we are to obey whatever he has called us to accomplish in the meantime.

*Lord, may I wait obediently in stillness*
*and in patience.*

4   Lisa Whittle, *Jesus over Everything: Uncomplicating the Daily Struggle to Put Jesus First* (Nashville, TN: Thomas Nelson, 2020), 127.

# 64

# I AM HERE

*Jesus spoke to them at once.*
*"Don't be afraid," he said.*
*"Take courage! I am here!"*
MARK 6:50 NLT

One year, we didn't make it to our church's Easter service. We had bought pretty clothes and had given the kids haircuts. Everyone bathed the night before, and we planned to have lunch at Grandma's house after the service. Then we woke up on Easter morning to discover that Lucas was sick.

My heart sank. I felt starved for my church community. My faith was parched for a fresh anointing, and I knew in my spirit that our Easter service was exactly what my weary soul needed.

As I went about the day, sulking around the house because we missed church yet again, I heard a still, small voice whisper, *I am here. I am here in the disappointment. I am here in your holy*

*obedience. I am here in the midst of germs. I am here in the messy*
*mundane. I am here in your ministry of caregiving. These offerings*
*of care and of laying down your own desires are evidence of my*
*broken body and shed blood. And because you reside in broken*
*spaces with me, you will reign in heavenly spaces beside me. A*
*resurrection always arrives after faithful obedience.*

Caregiving might seem tomblike when we isolate at home, feeling exhausted from managing all the tasks behind closed doors and serving those who cannot care for themselves. We might feel scared as we weather the storms of life. But take courage, for he is always present and ready to provide his comfort.

*Thank you, Jesus, for always being present.*

# 65

# REFRAME YOUR MINDSET

*Consider it pure joy, my brothers and sisters, whenever you face trials of many kinds, because you know that the testing of your faith produces perseverance.*

JAMES 1:2–3 NIV

Consider it pure joy." This isn't our favorite verse, is it? In fact, we kind of like to ignore this verse, don't we? I know I do, and surely, I can't be alone in this sentiment. It is not easy to frame our mindset around these two simple words: pure joy.

Consider your trials pure joy: the screaming, the aggression, the difficult behavior, and the lack of understanding, communication, resources, or support. Consider it pure joy to lift our loved one back into bed or feed her or bathe him or explain, yet again, who we are in relation to them. Consider it pure joy to manage our exhaustion, anxiety, and isolation daily. Pure joy as poison flows through an IV drip and into our loved one's body.

When I find myself less than joyful over my circumstances, I reflect for a moment and gaze at the "Holy Work" sign that hangs above Lucas's bed. Then I imagine my entrance into heaven one day and hearing my Savior say, *Well done, good and faithful servant.* This moment of reflection gives me the strength I need to reframe my mindset in light of eternity. Reframe my mindset to reflect one of "pure joy."

Whisper the words, *Pure joy. Pure joy. Pure joy.* Let these words sink deeply into your soul.

> *Father, I repent of the times when I do not consider my trials to be pure joy. Help me to reframe my mindset.*

# 66

# THE GREATEST LOVE

*"Greater love has no one than this:*
*to lay down one's life for one's friends."*
JOHN 15:13 NIV

I knelt to put Lucas's shoes on his feet before a romp at the park.
My worldly titles of author, speaker, and CEO bear no significance
to him. What does matter is that I continue to meet his needs:
changing his diapers, feeding, bathing, dressing him, and placing
shoes on his feet.

Jesus also knelt to serve, setting aside his titles: Messiah,
God, and Creator. He washed dirty feet, touched diseased skin,
associated with outcasts, and prostrated himself before humanity as
nails pierced his hands and his body lurched in agony. He humbled
himself before the least of these: the leper, the prostitute, the
crippled, the thief, and even you and me.

Jesus walked among the broken in body and in spirit; those who relied on the generosity of normal, everyday folks for their next meal; those who probably couldn't control their bladders or put shoes on without assistance or needed help dressing or bathing.

These monotonous, daily tasks are moments of holy annoyance: holy like washing filthy feet, holy like hanging out with lepers, holy like being broken and bruised for all. My Savior, who loved me in the most beautiful, humble, and miraculous way by laying down his life so that mine might be saved, considers my acts of service to Lucas as the greatest way to love.

*Thank you, Jesus, for the gift of my salvation. May I never forget and always strive to serve others with the same sacrificial love.*

# 67

# BLESSED

*"Blessed are the meek,*
*for they will inherit the earth."*
MATTHEW 5:5 NIV

Every year, without fail, August arrives. It's a month drenched
in personal significance. It's the month when Lucas was born and
the month when seven of our children said goodbye to either their
father or mother. Ryan's first wife had passed away from cancer too.

August is also a month of caregiving reminders and triggers.
A month of three stories—those of a father who fought cancer for
three years, a young mother who lost her battle after fighting for
mere months, and a little boy, the meekest of the meek, thriving
and spreading the message of hope with every breath he takes
more than twenty years after doctors declared him dead—each
intertwined to write a bigger story of sacrifice, surrender, and
symbolism. Sacrifice through years of caregiving. Surrender to

accept God's will. Eternal symbolism in witnessing the Lord's strength made perfect in our weakness.

God's ways are never our ways, *For I am God, and you are not,* thus sayeth the Lord of Hosts. Blessed are the meek. And the weak. And the lonely. And those gasping for one more breath. And those with IVs in their arms. And those swallowing big pills for their even bigger problems. And those steeped in depression. And those surviving on food stamps. And those writhing in addiction. And those who don't know if they can make it one more day.

Blessed are the single moms and the single dads. Blessed are those who cry out for relief, or live in the shadows, or weep beside a grave. Blessed are all the Lucases who came into this world defiantly screaming. And blessed are you, dear caregiver, the exhausted and sometimes forgotten one. Blessed are you, for you shall inherit the earth.

*Thank you, Lord, for the blessing in our meekness.*

# 68

# FEAR NOT

*"Fear not, for I am with you;*
*be not dismayed, for I am your God;*
*I will strengthen you, yes, I will help you,*
*I will uphold you with My righteous right hand."*
ISAIAH 41:10 NKJV

I received disturbing news that our county may change services for individuals like Lucas. Specifically, there was talk that the government would reduce services, such as day programs or employment options, for disabled adults as they age. These are desperately needed services for families like mine, services for which we specifically moved to Michigan.

Of course, I began to panic. I made a list of people to call. I brainstormed about starting a private school or a day program. I ranted to Ryan about how unfair it is that kids like Lucas always fall through the cracks and that parents like us always must fight for every single thing.

Then my husband suggested we claim God's promises over our situation. He opened his Bible and read, "Fear not, for I am with you; be not dismayed, for I am your God; I will strengthen you, yes, I will help you, I will uphold you."

I noticed the number of "I will" statements packed into that one little verse and realized I had a choice to make. If I believed God's promises, then I had to release my worry and trust that he would strengthen me, help me, and uphold me.

Do you also have a choice to make? Do you believe God will strengthen you, help you, and uphold you during this difficult season?

> *Lord, it can be difficult to truly trust you, but help me*
> *to believe that when you say you will do something,*
> *you will come through for me.*

# 69

# ALL THINGS FOR GOOD

*We know that for those who love God all things work together for good, for those who are called according to his purpose.*

ROMANS 8:28 ESV

Lucas woke at five in the morning after wetting through his pull-up. And because he was sleep-deprived, he opposed everything I tried to accomplish that morning before church. I finally managed to get him ready and coax him into the van, and I was exhausted by the time we arrived.

The pastor read from the Word, "We know that for those who love God all things work together for good."

I asked myself, *Do I believe this?* Sure, it's easy to be sincere about this verse when life is going according to plan, but what about my circumstances? What about my life?

How were things working together for good while I raised Lucas, who screamed at me at five in the morning and who fought me when I put on his socks and shoes? How was it "good" when Jason died from cancer, leaving me a widow with four young children?

The pastor closed his Bible and began to pray. Before bowing my head, I looked down the row at my six beautiful children and Ryan. I thought about Lucas, who was enjoying *Veggie Tales* in his special needs ministry, and his sister in her Sunday School classroom, a child born of my union with Ryan. Beauty from ashes. *Yes, Lord,* I whispered, *you do work all things together for good.*

*Father, help me to remember that you orchestrate all things for the good of those who put their trust in you.*

# 70

# GIVE US THIS DAY

*The Lord said to Moses, "I will rain down bread from heaven for you.*
*The people are to go out each day and gather enough for that day."*
EXODUS 16:4 NIV

When Lucas returned to school after summer break, I was unnerved by my lack of tasks and duties. Every thirty minutes, I would ignore the sounds around me to listen intently for him. Or I would look at the baby monitor only to find the screen empty. I would check for a diaper to change, but there wasn't one. Every couple of hours I would find myself in his room, having forgotten why I went there; my body couldn't forget the routine.

Mine is a common illustration of the type of post-traumatic stress that caregivers experience. It is a refining process—a constant laying down of our desires and a readiness to care for someone who's unable to care for themselves. It is a holy, exhaustive calling that requires patience and self-care and sometimes righteous anger and unrelenting faith—faith that there is meaning in our caregiving beyond ourselves.

And this faith keeps us moving forward in the monotony of tasks as we surrender to the process being worked out in our lives. Like yeast kneaded through dough, rising and falling and rising again, giving us our daily bread, this faith infuses us with renewed strength and peace.

Gloriously, the sun somehow appears—or maybe some days it doesn't—and we are greeted with the gift of time, bringing us fresh grace and new mercies served alongside lukewarm coffee. We offer a familiar prayer, *Give us this day our daily bread,* and we open our hands to receive fresh manna from heaven.

*Lord, thank you for your daily provisions.*

# 71

# REVEAL YOUR GLORY

*I consider that the sufferings of this present time are not worth comparing with the glory that is to be revealed to us.*
ROMANS 8:18 ESV

A few years ago, as Lucas lay quietly sedated in the intensive care unit after a shunt malfunction, I saw a glimpse of a different life. Not a life in ICU, surrounded by beeping machines and lifesaving equipment, but an easier, simpler life at home.

A life where I awoke to the rising sun instead of Lucas's screams over the baby monitor. A life where I had the freedom to run to the grocery store without worrying about who would stay home with my disabled son. A life where I didn't have to figure out what my nonverbal child wanted. A life void of diapers and wheelchairs and walls smeared with food. A more peaceful life. A life without Lucas.

Suffering has a way of forcing beauty to the surface. The pink cactus, planted in dry, parched land, sinks its roots deeply into the brittle soil, willing its way to the surface before its bright petals unfold in majestic glory. It reminds me of my life—unearthed through trauma and agony that brought me to my knees as I begged God to heal my son.

In my garden of Gethsemane, beside the cords and tubes and beeping machines, sweat dripping from my brow, I pleaded, *Father, grant me the strength to endure the suffering you have placed before me. Please spare my son and reveal your glory through us. Grant me the grace and the strength to walk the road.*

*Jesus, not my will but yours be done. Amen.*

# 72

# RESURRECTION

*"He is not here; he has risen, just as he said."*
MATTHEW 28:6 NIV

I remember the summer of 2010, the most difficult season of my life. Full of overwhelming obligations and demands, it was the summer I had to prepare a funeral for my young husband, the father of my children.

And today, as I care for my son, who becomes increasingly difficult to care for as he grows older, I remember this familiar soil—rich soil—like it was that summer of 2010, when perhaps I had not been buried but, instead, planted. I awaited my reemergence into the light, and I waited for a resurrection. I stayed faithful to what I had been called to do in that season of life, and today I do the same. I remain faithful and wait for my resurrection.

As believers, we have faith that a resurrection will occur for ourselves and for our loved ones because that's how this life gig works. It's how our human experience is rigged. Everything remains in motion: a continuous movement of death and life, waves washing away the brokenness and grief and pushing to the shore what remains.

It's all involved, collectively and individually; ashes to beauty and back to ashes again; circular movements until the Maestro sweeps his baton one last time and bows his head in holy reverence; that moment when his beloved creation leans into the finality of our experiences, and we release a labored breath, bursting into our ultimate resurrection. And that, dear caregiver, is where our eternal hope lies.

*Thank you, Jesus, for your resurrected power in my*
*life and in the lives of my loved ones.*

# 73

# STRENGTH FOR HARD TIMES

*I can do all things through him who strengthens me.*
PHILIPPIANS 4:13 ESV

A stack of papers sat on my desk for months during the summer of 2022. Papers I saw every day that went untouched. Papers that glistened with dusty sparkles as the sun played peekaboo through wispy curtains. Papers that would grant me guardianship over my adult son. Papers that I could not believe had crept their way into my life because I remembered playing peekaboo with my little boy like it was yesterday. Peekaboo with a child who had no interest in playing with me.

These papers told the truth: my caregiving role might never end, and I might never have an empty nest. They told me that I am Lucas's forever person, his caregiver, his mom, and his guardian. These papers freaked me out because it's a little bit scary to take away someone else's autonomy!

I avoided these papers for weeks (very un-Jessica-like) and finally prayed a simple prayer: *Lord, give me the courage I need to fill out these papers.* I coupled that prayer with action and sat down at the kitchen table, pen in hand. The Lord granted me the strength I needed to accomplish this difficult task.

In whatever life throws our way, we must find a way to move forward, for this is God's will for our lives. It is never his will that we get stuck in the hardships, but we can't move in our own strength. Everything we accomplish is because of God's strength in our lives.

*Lord, grant me your strength as I face the difficult tasks before me.*

# 74

# INTO THE ARK

*The L*ORD *then said to Noah, "Go into the ark, you and your whole*
*family, because I have found you righteous in this generation."*
GENESIS 7:1 NIV

Most days I awake in extreme pain. I feel it in my hips, back, and neck. This had been my story for over a year before I found hope on one late, late summer day.

I had done what I did most mornings: I got Lucas ready for school and on the bus, and then I laced up my shoes and embarked on a two-mile walk to loosen my joints and shake off the stress. As I walked, I glanced up at the bright blue sky and noticed leaves beginning to turn colors. They resembled a rainbow. I wept, thankful for the sunglasses that hid my vulnerability from cars whizzing by.

Being Lucas's mom has broken me in so many ways over the years—mentally, spiritually, emotionally, and, most profoundly, physically. My body is in constant pain even though I do a lot of things right. I eat healthy food, I work out, and I stretch. I see a chiropractor, I get acupuncture, and I must have spent at least a million dollars to date on supplements. I schedule massages and take vacations.

Still I live in pain. The specialists tell me to get my stress under control, *But how*, I wonder, *when I am a caregiver who lives in a perpetual state of fight or flight?*

As a few beautiful rainbow leaves cascaded around me, I was reminded of the Lord's faithfulness to another family once upon a time: *You are in the ark, my child, and I am faithful.*

Stay beside the Lord, and he will faithfully provide—even when the waters rise all around us.

*Thank you, Lord, for your promises.*

# 75

# PRUNING FOR REST

*"For six years you shall sow your field, and for six years you shall prune your vineyard and gather in its produce, but during the seventh year the land shall have a sabbath rest, a sabbath to the LORD."*

LEVITICUS 25:3–4 NASB

When we lived in Tennessee, I had the brilliant idea to plant grape vines. The first year, we saw nothing. The second year, we still saw nothing. The third year, there was tons of growth!

"Yay! It looks like we might see a few grapes this year!" I said excitedly to Ryan.

"Nope," my husband replied, "Not this year. This year we'll have to prune so that next year we can enjoy our harvest."

We did indeed prune those branches, but even the best-laid plans go awry sometimes. By the time fall arrived that year, the stress in our lives had become so overwhelming that Ryan lost twenty pounds. The weight loss happened in such a short period of time that it concerned his doctors, who wanted to schedule a PET scan.

"Jess," Ryan said, "the doctors think it might be cancer."

Fear and uncertainty hung in the air as we contemplated how overwhelming our life as caregivers had become. What could we say no to? What needed pruning?

Thankfully, the PET scan found nothing. Ryan's doctor attributed the rapid weight loss to the stress of caring for Lucas and admonished Ryan to make lifestyle changes to mitigate his anxiety. We prayed and knew it was time to say goodbye to our homestead—and the grapevines.

It can be difficult to recognize a need for rest, but a lack of rest quickly leads to negative consequences, such as stress and crankiness. Perhaps your life needs pruning, whether that's relocating like we did or investing in a grocery delivery service or ordering takeout once a week to relieve yourself of cooking.

Prune wherever you need to as you enter a season of harvest.

*Lord, help me to prune so that I can find rest.*

# FALL

*Let us not grow weary of doing good,*
*for in due season we will reap, if we do not give up.*
GALATIANS 6:9 ESV

Crisp, cool air ushers in the season of fall, and we embrace a bittersweet sense of normalcy.

We may feel increasingly hopeful while planning a future for our loved one and, in turn, a future for ourselves—a future that might include a residential facility, a nursing home, or an assisted living environment to grant us breaks from our caregiving duties. Or maybe we face a future without our loved one, leaving us to grapple with a new normal in their absence.

Fall is not a resignation but an acceptance of what is and what is not. Whatever the journey entails, we have learned, sometimes painfully, that we will make it through with the Lord's help. We've learned to trust our heavenly Father's overwhelming love for our loved one and for us.

# 76

# ALONE WITH OUR FATHER

*As soon as Jesus heard the news,*
*he left in a boat to a remote area to be alone.*

MATTHEW 14:13 NLT

After Jason's funeral, I drove home alone with my four fatherless children. Many people offered to accompany me, but I needed to process my grief and the tumultuous three-year journey I had traversed alone with my heavenly Father.

I desperately needed a renewal of body, soul, and spirit, which I knew I could only obtain through a period of rest and prayer with my Lord. After Jesus received the news that John the Baptist was beheaded, he also felt the need to be alone to process, grieve, and receive comfort from his Father.

There is a time to be surrounded by encouragement and comfort from loved ones, but their presence can, and does at times, delay what we need to face with our God.

When we realize that the time has come to meet with our Father and reflect—perhaps after the death of a loved one or maybe after we admit them to a group home or assisted living, whatever period of grief we find ourselves in—let's allow the Lord to comfort us in a remote spot, alone. Not only do we process our grief in this solitude, but we also receive the Lord's comfort, the ultimate healing balm.

*Father, may we remember to reserve space for you alone to comfort and heal our broken hearts.*

# 77

# A SURRENDERED HALLELUJAH

*Naked came I out of my mother's womb, and naked shall I return thither: the LORD gave, and the LORD hath taken away; blessed be the name of the LORD.*

JOB 1:21 KJV

The morning after Jason's death, I posted the following words on my blog:

> Jason Thomas Crisman received his final treatment last night when he was escorted into the arms of the Ultimate Healer. Praise God, this treatment wiped the cancer out of his body completely. He is now healed and whole. I told him, I'll see you soon...But not too soon. I'm so happy he's not in pain anymore yet so lonely at the reality that I've lost my best friend, my husband, and the father of my children. The Lord gives and the Lord takes away. Blessed be the name of the Lord.

There was nothing left to say. I bowed my head in reverence and submitted my surrendered hallelujah to the Lord.

There comes a point in the caregiving journey when we have to make a choice. We either bow our will in holy acknowledgment that God is God and we are not and blessed be his name, or we grow bitter and resentful.

If we bow in reverence to his sovereignty, it is within our surrender that the Holy Spirit rushes in to fill us with peace. We receive a peace that surpasses understanding when we acknowledge our limited understanding and accept his ultimate will, even unto death.

*Holy Spirit, as I surrender, fill me with a peace that passes understanding.*

# 78

# LIVE IN THE PRESENT

*Lot's wife looked back,*
*and she became a pillar of salt.*
GENESIS 19:26 NIV

When the Lord destroyed the evil cities of Sodom and Gomorrah, he spared Lot and his wife from destruction; however, the heavenly messengers had one stipulation: Lot and his wife were to leave and not look back when they departed. Lot obeyed. His wife did not, and she immediately turned into a pillar of salt.

It's easy and sometimes even tempting to wallow in painful what-ifs of the past: What if my child were normal? What if I had never eaten deli meat when I was pregnant? What if I had been diagnosed sooner? What if Jason had never drunk all those energy drinks?

But the bigger truth we must understand is that we become stagnant and lifeless, like a pillar of salt, when we dwell on pointless hypothetical questions.

We can't return to the past, nor can we resurrect it. We will find neither God nor life in our past; he resides in the present. When we forget this truth and yearn for what we cannot have and what will never be, it means we no longer trust the Lord. We instead worship ourselves as wannabe gods, entertaining thoughts like, *I wouldn't have let the cancer grow. I would have healed him here on earth, and I would have allowed us to stay in Sodom.*

The I-Would-Have game doesn't end well. Face forward and walk toward the land of the living. Like Lot, walk toward life.

*Lord, I choose to live in the present with you.*

# 79

# STRONG REFUGE

*The LORD is good, a strong refuge when trouble comes.*
*He is close to those who trust in him.*

NAHUM 1:7 NLT

Frantic and desperate for community, we left our rural home in Tennessee over the kids' Thanksgiving break to move closer to Nashville. We pulled the kids out of school, packed up our eight children and seven years' worth of life, and left—even before our house sold.

Ryan and I felt an overwhelming pressure to leave quickly. The never-ending demands of caregiving were deteriorating his health, and I was not in a good place mentally or emotionally. We needed hope like we needed oxygen.

Three weeks later, Lucas was in the ICU, which became a six-week stay for a shunt malfunction. Four weeks after that, our old home in rural Tennessee suffered a record-breaking flood in the backyard, which shut down all power for weeks.

However, because we now lived closer to Nashville, we were only thirty minutes away from the hospital versus three hours had we still lived in rural Tennessee. We would have been without power for weeks with an autistic son who lives for his iPad. Four months later, the pandemic hit.

God knew what he was doing by placing a spirit of urgency in us. We didn't necessarily understand, but we obeyed. He remained close to us and saved us from trouble before we even knew that trouble was on the horizon.

Trust that he is going before you, and he will provide a strong refuge in your time of need.

*Thank you, Lord, for going before us and for paving the way even when we don't understand.*

# 80

# GOD OF ALL COMFORT

*Blessed be the God and Father of our Lord Jesus Christ, the Father of mercies and God of all comfort, who comforts us in all our affliction.*

2 CORINTHIANS 1:3–4 ESV

R yan and I recently tried something new: a fun family movie night. We ordered pizza, purchased a movie, and popped popcorn, and the kids invited their friends. Unfortunately, Lucas made the night absolutely miserable.

We invited Lucas to participate, but he wanted his normal routine of enjoying his iPad while sitting alongside a companion—usually his brother—in his tattered brown chair in his room. But on this night, his brother wanted to participate in family movie night.

Upset and screaming, Lucas ascended and descended the stairs and yanked our arms. In Lucas's world, there is no compromise, no explanations, and no wiggle room. He demanded his normal, so I had to miss out on movie night and sit beside him.

I had to sacrifice a rare opportunity for family time to be a caregiver once again. And again, and again, and again.

I whispered under my breath a thousand frustrations and not-fairs, dwelling on the injustice of our reality that forces Ryan and me to divide and conquer.

Then a still, small voice whispered, *I am here. I am your comforter. You are doing holy work, holy kingdom-building work, and you are serving me as you serve your son. I will breathe peace into your weary, angry, and frustrated spaces.*

With the Lord's encouragement, I wrapped my arms around my grown boy, led him to his tattered chair, cued up *Veggie Tales* on his iPad, and exhaled into my heavenly Father's comfort once again.

*Holy Spirit, breathe peace into weary, angry, and frustrated spaces.*

# 81

# OUT OF THE HOUR

*"My soul is troubled, and what shall I say? 'Father, save me from this hour'? No, it was for this very reason I came to this hour. Father, glorify your name!"*

JOHN 12:27–28 NIV

I begged God to save me from having to raise a disabled child. On May 30, 2004, just months before I gave birth to Lucas, I wrote in my journal, "At dinner tonight I saw an older girl in a wheelchair acting like a two-year-old and drinking from a sippy cup. I don't think I can handle that scenario, yet I want to be faithful to whatever God has for me."

I received my worst-case scenario, and God was faithful. I asked (begged!) to be saved from having to be the mother of a profoundly disabled child, and the Lord said no. God has used that *no* in ways I could have never imagined on that difficult day in 2004.

Oswald Chambers says our Lord was saved "not from the hour, but out of the hour."[5] Suffering is part of the human experience. We are not saved from our caregiving duties, but we will have the strength to fulfill them when we place our faith in God. And when we do this, we rise. We don't get out of the suffering; we get through the suffering, and our resurrection brings help and hope to others.

*Lord, save us not from the hour but out of the hour,*
*and may our suffering bring glory to your name.*

---

5  Chambers, "Receiving One's Self in the Fires of Sorrow," *My Utmost for His Highest*, June 25.

# 82

# CAMPING BEFORE CROSSING

*Early in the morning Joshua and all the Israelites set out from Shittim and went to the Jordan, where they camped before crossing over.*

JOSHUA 3:1 NIV

When we uprooted our lives and moved to Nashville, Tennessee, from rural Tennessee, Ryan and I thought for sure, *This is it*. We were going to live in Nashville forever and find the resources we needed for Lucas. And then a global pandemic hit, and Nashville had no more resources than rural Tennessee, so we reluctantly moved again to my hometown in Michigan.

We often wondered about the purpose of our two-year stint in Nashville, but in hindsight, we see how God was faithful. Had we moved to Michigan before Nashville, we would have been stuck indoors with eight children and one with autism during a bitterly cold winter and during a pandemic. Instead, our children enjoyed warm weather and open parks in Tennessee.

We had to patiently camp by the river before we could move into the blessing that the Lord had prepared for us, where we would find support in our caregiving journey. And he was faithful. We even made a profit on a house we had lived in for only two years.

If you are in a waiting period, remember the Israelites. They camped for a period of time before they were ready to cross over into the promised land. Sometimes we're waiting for healing. Sometimes we're waiting for a revelation, and sometimes, we might be waiting for death.

Only God knows what the waiting period is about, but trust him. Our job is to patiently wait and trust that the Lord will move in our lives in his timing, not ours.

*Lord, give me patience as I wait.*

# 83

# NO CONDEMNATION

*There is therefore now no condemnation
for those who are in Christ Jesus.*
ROMANS 8:1 ESV

As caregivers, we often change protocols or situations when they no longer work for us. Maybe it's a treatment or a medication, or perhaps your loved one isn't thriving at home and it's time to consider assisted living. As we grow, we view situations differently. Our black-and-white perspectives might become a little more gray once we understand that most issues are more circular and not so linear.

I swore I'd never resort to medication for Lucas; however, during the pandemic, I changed my mind, and meds proved to be a game changer! His anxiety decreased significantly, and he began to speak more. Then I struggled with the guilt of *Why hadn't I tried meds sooner?*

I've also shared about how I believed I would be Lucas's forever caregiver, but as he aged and became more difficult, I thought about a different path. That path led to the creation of Hope Farm, and yes, there are feelings of guilt as I prepare to release my boy into the world. Both decisions were steeped in a fear of the unknown, and it was my love that prevented me from trying something new.

We deeply love the ones we care for, but sometimes we make mistakes when it comes to their best interests. We need to give ourselves grace and accept that our mistakes came from a place of love, and there is no condemnation where love abounds. We can reframe our stories and see our changed perspectives as a sign of growth and maturity.

*Lord, I am thankful that there is no condemnation*
*for those who place their hope in you.*

# 84

# SACRIFICE

*"Do not lay your hand on the boy or do anything to him, for now I know that you fear God, seeing you have not withheld your son, your only son, from me."*

GENESIS 22:12 ESV

W hen Lucas was an adorable little boy, I believed I would be his caregiver forever. I believed this until he blossomed into manhood and grew larger, stronger, and aggressive at times. I cried out, *Lord! I don't know how to surrender Lucas to you! I'm his mom! I need to make sure he's safe!*

But a still, small voice replied, *If you don't trust me with Lucas, you have made caring for him your idol.* Ouch. I slowly began to release Lucas's life to his Creator. After more than nineteen years of sacrifice for my son, I continue to surrender him to the Lord's care, as Abraham did with Isaac.

We caregivers intimately understand the concept of sacrifice. We sacrifice our agendas, vacations, and date nights. We sacrifice time spent with friends and family. Most of us are acutely aware of the sacrifices we have made and continue to make for our loved ones, but would we sacrifice our caregiving role if the Lord asked us to? Or are we so wrapped up in our role as caregivers that it has become our identity?

These are hard, holy questions we must face as we let go of our tendency to make an idol of our caregiving duties. We must walk in obedience to God's will even though it's hard. It's hard, *and* it's necessary.

*Lord, I completely surrender my loved one to your*
*care and whatever that may look like in the future.*

# 85

# CONFIRMATION

*Though the LORD gave you adversity for food and suffering for drink,*
*he will still be with you to teach you. You will see your teacher with*
*your own eyes. Your own ears will hear him. Right behind you a*
*voice will say, "This is the way you should go."*

ISAIAH 30:20–21 NLT

As Lucas grew up, I began to recognize that having said yes to being his sole caregiver for the rest of his life would require saying no to other aspects of my life, such as community, friendships, and travel.

Then one day, Lucas came home from school with a piece of paper that prompted him to indicate where he wanted to live when he became an adult. Lucas had circled the option "with my friends." With this revelation of his, I knew that he (and I) would live our best lives away from my 24/7 care. I intensely researched options: openings in group homes, waitlists, and services.

Then my realtor sent me a listing for a unique property that was on the market and just ten minutes away from our current home. The listing wasn't getting much interest because it had not one but two homes on the land. We toured it and knew immediately that this was Lucas's future home.

I requested that we sign the closing documents on Lucas's birthday, August 12, and when the realtor conveyed my request to the seller, the seller cried. Her birthday was also August 12.

Despite all the things I have had to say no to over the years, the Lord confirmed that yes, this was the way we should go.

*Lord, help me have eyes to see and ears to hear your confirmation in my life.*

# 86

# BOLDLY ASK

*"Lord," they answered, "We want our sight!"*
*Jesus had compassion on them and touched their eyes.*
*Immediately they received their sight and followed him.*
MATTHEW 20:33–34 NIV

Isn't this exchange between two blind guys and Jesus the best? These men encountered Jesus, who asked what he could do for them. They boldly declared that they wanted to be able to see, and boom! Their eyesight was immediately restored. Imagine what this miracle must have felt like for them.

I spent years worrying about Lucas's future. I tossed and turned at night, attempting to develop a solution and wondering who would take care of him once I was gone. I asked myself if I should discuss Lucas's future care with his siblings or with our friends and family.

Then one day I chose to be bold and simply prayed, *Lord, I need a solution for my son's future.* Direct and honest. Six months later we signed closing papers for Hope Farm, and I felt a little bit like those blind guys who asked Jesus to restore their sight.

God's Word promises, "Ask, and it shall be given you; seek, and ye shall find; knock, and it shall be opened unto you" (Matthew 7:7 KJV). Boldly ask the Lord for what you need. His answers might not arrive exactly as you want or when you want them to, but trust that his providence far exceeds anything our human capacity can imagine.

He is willing and able to provide, but you must ask.

*Lord, help us to ask with boldness and then to trust*
*you will provide according to your perfect plan.*

# 87

# THINGS NOT YET SEEN

*By faith Noah, being warned of God of things not seen as yet, moved with fear, prepared an ark to the saving of his house; by the which he condemned the world, and became heir of the righteousness which is by faith.*

HEBREWS 11:7 KJV

I recently stumbled across a notebook I had forgotten about. While thumbing through the pages, I paused and smiled. I had lists of thoughts pertaining to a future residential home for Lucas. There were pictures and sketches of what that dream would look like and budgets breaking down the cost. There were fundraising and direct care ideas. There were also Bible verses scribbled throughout the pages, verses such as the one for today.

Notice the phrase "moved with fear." Noah wasn't fearless when God warned him. No, he acted despite his fear, and God still blessed him. I, too, acted despite my fear about Lucas's future, and the Lord faithfully prepared a way for us to create Hope Farm.

When God places a dream in your heart, claim it. Write about it, speak about it, dream about it, and then marvel at the awesomeness of our God when he provides a boat in the middle of a flood.

What's your Noah dream? Are you stepping forward in faith and obedience to accomplish it? Has the Lord called you to a "crazy obedience" like he did with Noah or with me with Hope Farm? Hold fast to the seed he planted in your heart. If he sees you to it, he will see you through it.

*Lord, I believe in the dreams you have placed*
*in my heart. Give me the perseverance to see*
*them through.*

# 88

# SEVEN TIMES

*Nebuchadnezzar was furious with Shadrach, Meshach and Abednego, and his attitude toward them changed. He ordered the furnace heated seven times hotter than usual and commanded some of the strongest soldiers in his army to tie up Shadrach, Meshach and Abednego and throw them into the blazing furnace.*

DANIEL 3:19–20 NIV

As the early morning sun peeked through the curtains, I poured five gallons of sap into a large pot, turned the igniter to high, and eagerly anticipated the maple syrup I'd later enjoy. Ryan and I discovered that we have about fifteen maple trees at Hope Farm, and we enjoyed learning how to make syrup.

I finished my kitchen duties, poured myself a steaming cup of coffee, and sat down to read my devotions. I read, "He ordered the furnace heated seven times hotter than usual."

I paused and underlined *seven*. How often had I felt the heat increase at least seven times before experiencing a breakthrough, especially through my years of caregiving? According to biblical history, the number seven symbolizes completion, rest, and victory, all of which I've experienced when the number seven has shown up in my life.

Before I began my workday, I grabbed the thermometer and set the alarm to sound when the sap reached 212 degrees. It would take six hours to reach this temperature, and then, during the seventh hour, once it hit 212, it would quickly increase to 219: the temperature of completion for maple syrup.

Sometimes the heat must increase seven times before something reaches completion or before our rescue arrives. Has the heat increased in your life? Stay faithful. The process hasn't reached its completion yet.

*Thank you, Lord, for providing a rescue when we*
*stay faithful and obedient.*

# 89

# OBEDIENCE

*It is God which worketh in you
both to will and to do of his good pleasure.*

PHILIPPIANS 2:13 KJV

**W**hat does it mean to work out our salvation? What determines
faith? Or godliness? What is the "it" factor that David, a man after
God's own heart, possessed? Or Enoch, who walked with God
and then was no more? Or Mary, supernaturally impregnated and
carrying the Messiah within her womb? The more I meditate on
these individuals, the more clearly I see that everything is tied to
obedience, to actions intertwined with forward movement.

Obedience is the barometer of faithfulness and can even
overshadow character flaws and bad choices. God often requires
this obedience in the face of a seemingly ridiculous request, a
request that the rest of the world might find unbelievable and

absurd, a request that, quite likely, requires brash courage and thick skin because the naysayers will have some naysaying, for sure.

God has asked me to obey ridiculous requests: carry a terminal baby and then care for a child who cannot care for himself. My resolve has wavered, but a protection of grace arises out of obedience, obedience in spite of my stubbornness, mouthiness, know-it-all attitude, grumbling, and, at times, bad choices. Every action is either obedience toward his perfect will or disobedience to what he's called me to do.

And the working out part? That's where (hopefully) the character flaws, personality quirks, and bad attitudes start to iron out. Choice by choice, we walk in his purpose and plan, and that is where we find the sweet spot, that place of peace and rest, even in the middle of our caregiving lives.

*Lord, may I walk in obedience to your perfect will.*

# 90

# HELP FROM THE HOLY SPIRIT

*"The Helper, the Holy Spirit, whom the Father will send in My name, He will teach you all things, and bring to your remembrance all things that I said to you."*

JOHN 14:26 NKJV

If I'm being entirely honest, the concept of the Holy Spirit has often been an area of concern for me. I had no problem accepting God the Father or Jesus Christ his Son, but the Holy Ghost was a bit of a mystery. A mystery I wasn't so sure about.

I grew up in a Pentecostal church, and I witnessed experiences attributed to the Holy Spirit that were strange. I'm not going to judge whether the Spirit was authentically moving during these moments; however, these incidents did cause some discomfort for an individual who is more conservatively inclined and not super demonstrative.

As Lucas has gotten older, somewhere in my desperation, the Holy Spirit and I became better acquainted. And then we became friends. In my darkest hours of worry over Lucas's future, the Spirit guided and comforted me as I grieved the process of accepting a future for him away from our home. The Holy Spirit provided clarity for the path forward when I was confused.

I have learned, ever so slowly, to surrender to the Spirit's lead in all areas of my life, and when I arrive at the end of myself, the Holy Spirit provides an ever-present source of help in my times of need.

*Holy Spirit, breathe your conviction, comfort, and clarity into my times of distress.*

# 91

# BELLY OF A WHALE

*"Salvation comes from the LORD."*
*And the LORD commanded the fish,*
*and it vomited Jonah onto dry land.*

JONAH 2:9–10 NIV

Jonah was stubborn and did not want to preach in Nineveh as the Lord had commanded him. He whined and bargained and finally ran away to where he thought the Lord wouldn't be able to reach him. Of course, God was still present, and Jonah found himself inside the belly of a whale. So absurd and so like God.

I was similarly stubborn and did not want to raise a disabled child. I ran away to rural Tennessee, a metaphorical belly of a whale. Between our profoundly disabled child and our beautiful home resting on thirty acres of land, our circumstances became overwhelmingly difficult and reeked of isolation. We surrendered to the Lord and to our reality, and we moved to my home state of Michigan.

When we surrender, God uses our stories to reach people for his kingdom. It wasn't until Jonah surrendered and declared that his salvation "comes from the LORD" that the Lord ordered the whale to spit Jonah out onto the beach. Then Jonah obeyed and preached to Nineveh as God had instructed him. God used the experiences of two stubborn people, Jonah and me, to humble us.

Are you inside the metaphorical belly of a whale? If so, what do you need to surrender? Release it and experience the spiritual shift that occurs when you let go.

*Lord, you alone are my salvation. I pray for a release in my circumstances.*

# 92

# HIDDEN BLESSINGS

*"I gave you a land on which you did not toil and cities you did not build; and you live in them and eat from vineyards and olive groves that you did not plant."*

JOSHUA 24:13 NIV

In 2008, I planted grape vines at Baylor Pond, the dream house I had built with Jason in Michigan. After Jason died, I moved to Wilderness Lane with my expanded family, where I planted grape vines with Ryan. And then we moved to rural Tennessee, where we planted chardonnay grapevines, which Ryan said would never survive because Tennessee is not known for chardonnay.

Then we moved to Nashville, where I planted more grape vines over the pergola in the backyard. And after the pandemic, we moved back to Michigan, where our new house is too shady for grapevines. I have never harvested a single grape from any of these efforts.

On August 12, 2022, we purchased Hope Farm for Lucas, and God smiled upon me and threw in an entire vineyard, one that we never planted or tended, a vineyard overflowing with grapes, so many grapes that we couldn't even make use of them all! We made wine and grape jelly and grape juice until our fingers were stained with purple.

The Lord sees our faithful obedience and rewards us with blessings that we cannot even comprehend or imagine. Great is his faithfulness.

*Thank you, Lord, for caring about the little things in life like grapevines.*

# 93

# SMALL AND INWARD

*Jesus said, "Let's go off by ourselves to a quiet place and rest awhile." He said this because there were so many people coming and going that Jesus and his apostles didn't even have time to eat.*

MARK 6:31 NLT

The Lord has been impressing upon me a desire to make my personal circle small and trustworthy while I work to accomplish a few big tasks he's called me to. These tasks require an immense amount of energy and focus, and I simply don't have much of either left to cultivate new relationships or begin extracurricular activities.

I found myself in a similar season when I was pregnant with Lucas. I surrounded myself with a trusted group of friends who encouraged me as we feasted on the Lord's Word and drank from his Spirit. And in doing so, I was equipped and strengthened for the task that was soon to arrive: being Lucas's mom.

If you're feeling a pull toward getting away from the hustle and bustle and leaning into a sacred space with a trusted community, remember that our Lord also felt this pull and found a quiet place where he rested with his disciples.

We simply don't have the capacity to do everything, and as we serve in these spaces of care, we require rest, like Jesus did. We require times of refreshment in order to recharge when life isn't so overwhelmingly hectic, and then we can reenter our ministry of caregiving with renewed strength and joy.

*Lord, may we remember to go small and inward as*
*we prioritize seasons of rest in our busy lives.*

# 94

# THE ANOINTING

*The LORD said, "Arise, anoint him, for this is he." Then Samuel took
the horn of oil and anointed him in the midst of his brothers. And
the Spirit of the LORD rushed upon David from that day forward.*

1 SAMUEL 16:12–13 ESV

About a week after I gave birth to Lucas, I felt the spirit
impressing upon me that I would one day start a nonprofit in his
honor. I had no idea when, where, or how this would occur, but I
felt an anointing in that sacred moment that my dream would one
day come to pass. And it did. Sixteen years later I started The Lucas
Project.

David was also anointed at a young age to become king;
however, he had to care for sheep for years before he saw the
anointing come to fruition and he could step into his kingdom
blessing. He obediently cared for his flock, which I imagine is a
much more difficult calling than caring for our loved ones. Through

David's faithful obedience, the Lord was glorified when David defeated Goliath and stepped into his reign as king.

Sometimes God gives us an anointing for a certain task, but we first have to prove ourselves faithful in the ordinary, everyday tasks before the blessing comes to pass. Has the Lord planted a seed in your heart? Stay faithful to what he has called you to accomplish in the present, and you will walk in his anointing in his timing.

*Lord, may we trust your timing when we sense an anointing on our lives.*

# 95

# HE IS WILLING

*Jesus reached out with His hand and touched him, saying, "I am willing; be cleansed." And immediately his leprosy was cleansed.*
MATTHEW 8:3 NASB

I definitely had my ideas of healing for Jason and Lucas. I wanted Lucas to be completely healed, mentally and physically, here on earth. I wholeheartedly believed that my will aligned with God's will, but it did not.

I also wanted Jason to be healed completely here on earth. The Lord was willing to heal them both, but not in the way I desired. Jason was healed in heaven, and though Lucas did not receive his healing the way that I envisioned, I now believe that he is exactly the way he is supposed to be.

The purpose, I believe, of these two vastly different circumstances was more about healing me than healing them. I needed healing from my preconceived ideas of what healing entailed and from my need to control every situation. I needed healing from my ego. I needed healing from viewing God as my personal magician who could miraculously fix all my problems when I spoke it and believed it.

Healing is never about whether the Lord is willing; it is about whether we are willing to accept his version of healing, which might not align with ours. Release your will for your loved one and be willing to accept healing however the Lord manifests it in your life.

*Lord, we praise you for your willingness to heal.*
*Please help us surrender to your perfect plan.*

# 96

# RELEASING OUR LOVED ONES

*When she could hide him no longer, she got a papyrus basket for him and coated it with tar and pitch. Then she placed the child in it and put it among the reeds along the bank of the Nile.*

EXODUS 2:3 NIV

When Lucas was three, we were offered the option of school. I yearned for a break, but he was only three! How could I release him into the world at such a young age?

I entered a season of prayer and felt peace about sending him for two days instead of five. Early that first morning, I waved goodbye as the bus departed and then spent the day worrying. I called the school to make sure he was okay, and they reassured me that he was.

I can't imagine the anguish that Moses' mother felt as her daughter, Miriam, released her son down the river. I'll bet she was a nervous wreck as she prayed for Moses, but she placed her trust in the Lord. She didn't focus on her feelings but instead focused on the one who would protect her baby boy.

As I began to trust the process of school, I added another day, and before I knew it, I was confidently sending Lucas five days a week and enjoying a break from my intense caregiving duties.

I'm revisiting these lessons as I prepare to release my boy down the river and into the world of adulthood. I am learning to trust that the Lord will protect him as God protected him at school and as he protected baby Moses many years ago.

*Lord, help us to trust the plan you place in our heart and then to move confidently into the process.*

# REDEMPTION

*Praise the LORD...who redeems your life from the pit
and crowns you with love and compassion.*

PSALM 103:2, 4 NIV

I often refer to myself as a reluctant caregiver. Never in a million years would I have imagined myself becoming a "voice for caregivers." I'm not super empathetic or sympathetic. I would make a horrible nurse. When my children are sick, I'm more of a "Here's your bucket and Sprite. Let me know if you need something" kind of mother rather than a "Let's cuddle all day" type. If I were God (and thankfully I am not), I would not look down from heaven and decide, *Yes! Jess Ronne, she's the one to become a caregiver!*

But the Lord, in his great mercy and wisdom, saw fit to tag me as a caregiver, and here I am, using my experiences to encourage and support those who are still in the pit. I've been able to use my experiences to bring water to those in need, which is a beautiful illustration of how the Lord can transform our pit of misery into a well of living water for others.

Do you allow the Lord to use your difficult caregiving experiences to bring hope to others? Or perhaps you are in a place where you need all the living water you can find.

I pray that the Lord sends help, but if you find in the future that you have been nourished and refreshed, pass that nourishment along. Become a well for those who are still on fire. Allow the Lord to redeem your story and your life.

*Father, thank you for those whom you have sent into my life to provide living water for my times of hardship.*

# 98

# MADE FOR ETERNITY

*He has made everything appropriate in its time.*
*He has also set eternity in their heart.*

ECCLESIASTES 3:11 NASB

There's a reason our souls cry out against our personal sufferings. There's a reason we weep in anguish over isolation and despair, and there's a reason our bodies ache in quiet despondency. We were not created for this sinful world and its hardships; we were made for eternity. This is why our souls long and ache for healing for our loved ones and why we yearn for reprieve.

When we view our lives and their circumstances from a purely human perspective, we focus on the despair, the diagnosis, or the death. We see aggressive behaviors emerging and medications failing and hair falling out. We lose hope.

In order to cultivate an eternal perspective, we must reframe the narrative. Instead of seeing Lucas as broken, I shifted my perspective to see him exactly as the person God wants him to be: a vessel bringing glory to God. Instead of seeing Jason as deceased, I shifted my perspective to view him as eternally healed and whole.

God has promised that he will make everything appropriate in its time, and this includes bringing an end to our suffering. For those of us who put our trust in the Lord, our hearts yearn for this perfection that we'll enjoy in heaven, when all will be made right again.

Hold fast to your yearning for something more, for those nudges are gentle reminders that challenging times will not last forever. He has promised that everything will be made right in his time.

*Thank you, Lord, for setting eternity in our hearts as a reminder that this world is not our home.*

# 99

# FOR I KNOW

*"I know the plans I have for you," declares the L*ORD*,*
*"plans to prosper you and not to harm you,*
*plans to give you hope and a future."*

JEREMIAH 29:11 NIV

W hen Jason was admitted to hospice, a friend stopped by with a meal. As we sat together and discussed how I was doing and how the kids were holding up, she asked if she could pray for me. As she prayed, she declared, *May Jess know that you have a plan for her, plans to prosper her and not to harm her, plans to give her a hope and a future.*

As my husband moaned in agony in the den and my infant son awoke from his nap, I felt tears threaten to spill over. The weight of my friend's words felt heavy and untrue. I couldn't imagine, in that moment, how there could be any hope or future worth squat coming out of my situation. I was about to lose my husband and become a single mom with four children under the age of seven.

But I was wrong. Six months later, I was engaged to Ryan, a widower who had three young children. The Lord did know the plans he had for me, and they included prosperity, hope, and a future, but I still had to wade through the pain, say goodbye to my husband, and mourn the life I believed I should have had.

How do you feel as you read this verse? Do you believe it? And if not, what's holding you back? He is a good God, and I promise he has a plan for your life.

*Father, help me to trust that you do have a good
plan for my life.*

# 100

# HOLD ON

*Sorrow and mourning will disappear,*
*and they will be filled with joy and gladness.*
ISAIAH 35:10 NLT

I recently found a calendar from 2010 and paused when I turned to August, each day overflowing: doctor's appointments, the arrival of hospice care, important phone calls, and goodbyes whispered to a young husband and father. It was the deepest season of sorrow and mourning I have ever experienced.

Years later on a fall morning, I bask in the warmth of the sun, a beautiful day spent watching my daughter fill her red wagon with dry, autumn leaves. A day I could not have imagined in my wildest dreams in August of 2010. A day saturated with joy and gladness.

The moral of the story? Circumstances can change in an instant. You may feel like you've been exiled from your life like the Israelites were, but hear me with this truth: hold on with every ounce of your being.

Hold on to he who is greater than he who is in the world. Hold on to that last shred of faith, no matter how unraveled or mangled it may seem. Hold on for goodness' sake and for every other sake, for you have no idea what's around the bend. You have no idea what may be in store for you when the Almighty flips your page or the blessing he may bestow when you fight the good fight and finish the race (2 Timothy 4:7).

You will have your joy and gladness; you will rise and have the crown of life bestowed upon your weary head, and you will hear those coveted words, *Well done, good and faithful servant.* I promise—your faithfulness will win in this life or the next as you enter your eternal homecoming.

*Lord, grant me the strength to hold on.*

# A Blessing for Caregivers

Father, bless and keep this beloved caregiver. May your glory shine down upon and around them and fill their weary spaces with hope. Keep them in the bosom of your care as they radiate your kingdom come in hard and holy moments. Use their skills for your glory and to further ignite the ultimate cause—grace heaped upon grace, reaching into the darkest crevices of servitude.

May they become a beacon of light as they enter the fellowship of care with their loved ones. Give them strength to serve as a battle shield against the weariness that will arise within the monotonous and mundane. Open their eyes to see beyond the present moment and firmly plant a vision of eternity in their hearts.

May they live to bring glory to your name until the day your heavenly angels escort them into your eternal presence, where they will hear the words that every servant of the Most High God yearns to hear: *Well done, good and faithful servant. Enter into your reward.*

To him be the glory, the honor, and the power forever and ever. Amen.

# ABOUT THE AUTHOR

Jessica Ronne calls herself "the reluctant caregiver" and believes that if she were the Almighty in search of a voice for caregivers, she would not have chosen herself!

But here she is in a role that has become strangely familiar, having cared for her sick husband for three years, her profoundly disabled son for more than nineteen years, eight children, and parent caregivers worldwide through her advocacy roles. It's not a position she would have ever picked, but it's a role that she has obediently embraced.

Though she admits she may not be the most sympathetic person, Jessica is a doer and a get-'er-done-r. She earned a master's degree in education from Grand Valley State University in 2015, walking the stage to accept the honor while seven months pregnant with her eighth child.

She is also the founder and executive director of The Lucas Project, a nonprofit serving parent caregivers with recognition, respite, and resources, and hosts *Coffee with Caregivers*, a podcast where she chats with caregivers about the joys and trials of raising a child with complex needs.

Drawing from her experiences as a caregiver, Jessica produced the documentary *Unseen: How We're Failing Parent Caregivers & Why It Matters*, which aired on PBS in 2023.

She is the creator of Hope Farm, a residential home for disabled adults, and author of *Sunlight Burning at Midnight*, *Blended with Grit and Grace*, *Lovin' with Grit & Grace*, and *Caregiving with Grit and Grace*.

Jessica believes that faithful obedience is what we are called to do on this side of eternity, and as long as she remains faithful, the Lord will provide. She and her husband, Ryan, reside in Holland, Michigan, with their children.

# About The Lucas Project

Founded by Jessica Ronne, The Lucas Project is a nonprofit organization providing recognition, respite, and resources to special needs families around the country.

The Lucas Project believes that the best way to support individuals with special needs is to support caregivers. To acknowledge their hard and holy work, The Lucas Project sends care packages with spa items, gourmet coffees and teas, and small, simple gifts.

The Lucas Project also offers free resources, such as The Lucas Project Resource Database and Caregiver's Cove, an online support group providing community, caregiver tips, informative videos, reading recommendations, recipes, and more.

Additionally, The Lucas Project purchased property in West Michigan to build an accessible respite facility, which will help the organization design and establish a facility model to offer nationwide.

To learn more about The Lucas Project, its mission, and how you can help, please visit the website at www.thelucasproject.org.

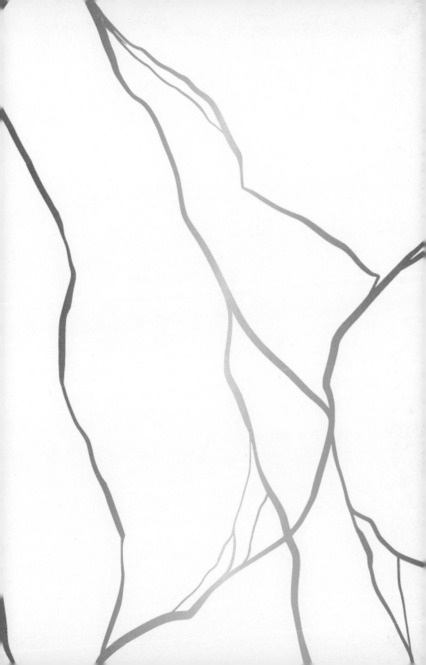